ISBN 978-0-282-49938-9
PIBN 10853858

1 MONTH OF
FREE
READING

at

www.ForgottenBooks.com

By purchasing this book you are eligible for one month membership to ForgottenBooks.com, giving you unlimited access to our entire collection of over 1,000,000 titles via our web site and mobile apps.

To claim your free month visit:

www.forgottenbooks.com/free853858

English
Français
Deutsche
Italiano
Español
Português

www.forgottenbooks.com

Mythology Photography **Fiction**
Fishing Christianity **Art** Cooking
Essays Buddhism Freemasonry
Medicine **Biology** Music **Ancient**
Egypt Evolution Carpentry Physics
Dance Geology **Mathematics** Fitness
Shakespeare **Folklore** Yoga Marketing
Confidence Immortality Biographies
Poetry **Psychology** Witchcraft
Electronics Chemistry History **Law**
Accounting **Philosophy** Anthropology
Alchemy Drama Quantum Mechanics
Atheism Sexual Health **Ancient History**
Entrepreneurship Languages Sport
Paleontology Needlework Islam
Metaphysics Investment Archaeology
Parenting Statistics Criminology
Motivational

THE COUNTRY HANDBOOKS—IV

Edited by Harry Roberts

The Still-Room

A CORNISH STILLER OF HERBS.

The Still-Room

By Mrs. Charles Roundell
and Harry Roberts

John Lane, The Bodley Head
London and New York MDCCCCIII

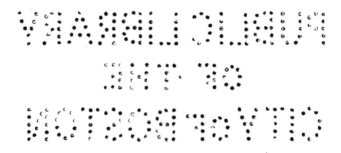
WILLIAM CLOWES AND SONS, LTD., LONDON AND BECCLES.

EDITOR'S NOTE

MRS. CHARLES ROUNDELL is responsible for the chapters dealing with the Pickling of Meat, Preserves, Refreshments at a Garden-Party, and Food for Invalids; as well as for certain recipes scattered through the book. These are distinguished by the initials "J. R."

CONTENTS

	Page
A Plea for Housewifery	1
Butter and Cream	9
Cheese	16
Pickling Meat	23
Fish	31
Eggs	32
Pickling Vegetables	33
Condiments and Sauces	40
Preserves	48
The Storing of Fruit and Herbs	57
The Bottling of Fruit and Vegetables	63
The Drying of Fruit and Vegetables	67
Home-brewed Beer	71
Cider	77
Wine-making	80
The Distilling of Waters and Cordials	92
Some other Cordials and Bitters	112
Drinks—Old and New	117
Hints for Refreshments at a Garden-party or Picnic	128
Ice Creams	137
Food for Invalids	139
Perfumes	145
Some Miscellaneous Recipes	149
Index	153

LIST OF ILLUSTRATIONS

A Cornish Stiller of Herbs . . . . Frontispiece

Symbols of Distillation . . . . . Page 3

Alchemist in his Laboratory . . . . „ 5

Alchemist performing Mystic Rites . . . „ 7

Diaphragm Churn . . . . . . „ 10

Melotte Cream Separator . . . . To face page 10

A Small Butter-worker . . . . . Page 11

Milk-Strainer for use with Muslin . . . „ 13

Double Pan for Devonshire Cream-raising . . „ 13

A Self-skimming Porcelain Milk-pan . . . „ 14

Butter-scoop . . . . „ 14

Old Distilling Furnaces and Stills . . . „ 35

Distilling Oyle out of Seedes . . . . „ 43

A Fruit-room . . . . „ 59

Orr's Fruit-storing Trays . . . . To face page 60

Lee's Steam Fruit Preserving Apparatus . „ „ 62

Ryland's Fruit Bottles . . . . . Page 64

Lee's Fruit Bottles and Boiler . . . To face page 64

Barnett and Foster's Spile-drawer . . . Page 74

A Group of Drinking-glasses . . . . „ 82

A Group of Ancient Bottles . . . . „ 83

A Simple Fruit-mill . . . . . . „ 84

Cork-driver . . . . „ 84

A Group of Modern Bottles . . . . „ 86

A Wine Filter-bag . . . . . . „ 88

Balneum Mariæ . . . . . . „ 93

xi

List of Illustrations

DISTILLING BY HEAT OF STEAM . . . . *Page* 93

SOME OLD DISTILLING VESSELS . . . . ,, 95

DISTILLING BY HEAT OF FERMENTING MANURE . . ,, 97

ALCHEMIST WITH HIS SERVANT . . . . ,, 97

A 16TH-CENTURY STILL, WITH CONDENSER JACKET
TO HELM OF STILL . . . . . ,, 99

"THE INSTRUMENT NAMED THE PELLICAN" . . ,, 99

STILLS AT THE WORKS OF THE LONDON ESSENCE CO. *To face page* 100

BALNEUM MARIÆ . . . . *Page* 101

FURNACE WITH STILLS . . . . . . ,, 101

STILL-ROOM OF THE LONDON ESSENCE CO. . *To face page* 102

FURNACE WITH STILLS . . . . . . *Page* 103

PERSIAN ROSE-WATER SPRINKLER . . . . ,, 104

A PERFORATED WATER-BATH . . . . . ,, 105

A PORTABLE COPPER STILL . . . . . ,, 105

OLD APPARATUS USED FOR CONDENSING THE DISTILLATE ,, 107

"BEHOLDE HERE A MANNER OR FASHION OF BALNEO
MARIÆ" . . . . ,, 109

OLD VESSELS USED IN DISTILLING . . . . ,, 110

TENDING THE FURNACE . . . . . . ,, 110

BALNEUM MARIÆ . . . . ,, 110

COPPER SPIRIT-MEASURE . . . . . . ,, 115

COPPER FUNNEL . . . . ,, 115

COFFEE ROASTER . . . . . . *To face page* 120

BEER WARMER OR MULLER . . . . . *Page* 122

SOME OLD MORTARS . . . . . . ,, 131

PERSIAN INCENSE BURNER . . . . . ,, 147

The Still-Room

"*The preparation of meats and bread and drinks, that they may be rightly handled, and in order to this intention, is of exceedingly great moment; howsomever it may seem a mechanical thing and savouring of the kitchen and buttery, yet it is of more consequence than those fables of gold and precious stones and the like.*"—BACON.

The
STILL-ROOM

A PLEA FOR HOUSEWIFERY

WE live in an age which may well be called the age of the purveyor; and, if we continue travelling along the road upon which we have entered, the time cannot be far distant when it will be held ridiculous to do anything at all for ourselves. To appreciate, to criticize, to display taste in selection —these are the hall-marks of to-day, and home is but another name for a private restaurant. Homes such as those in which Goldsmith and Dickens delighted are now calculated to bring a blush to the cheeks of the superior and the " artistic." Of few of our fine ladies can it be said that " they are excellent Housewives, and as capable of descending to the kitchen with propriety as of acting in their exalted stations with dignity."

We are nowadays far more willing to applaud and reward the woman who throws her " Letters " —real or imaginary—before the eyes of the bored and lazy world, than the one who is merely efficient in the sphere allotted to her sex by nature. An occasional grant, such as Stow records as being made by Henry VIII., would do much to remedy the position of the housewife. King Henry's grant was of an estate in Leadenhall Street to " *Mistris Cornewallies, widdow, and her heires, in reward of Fine Puddings by her made.*"

But suppers have gone out—not the midnight meals of the Strand and Piccadilly—cider has gone out, and home-cured hams, with home-brewed ale and home-stilled cordials, have gone the way of Mrs. Primrose's gooseberry wine and Mr. Frank Churchill's spruce beer.

Little economies are now as unfashionable as quiet generosity, hospitality, and comfort. If it is not beneath the dignity of a man to spend enjoyable hours of labour in laboratory or malthouse, in sick-ward or workshop, woman need not feel degraded by the apportionment to her of those duties which are more immediately bound up with the creation of happy and refreshing homes.

A private latch-key is no doubt part of the universal birthright, but it does not in itself afford a sufficient aim in life. To be able to discourse cleverly of Browning and Wagner is an accomplishment easily acquired, and affords pleasure to no one. To acquire a reputation for the excellence of our home-made gooseberry wine, of our home-baked bread, or of our home-brewed beer is much more difficult and much more worthy. There is more scope for the use of brains in housewifery than in almost any of the other careers open to women, and this possibly is why so many women are

SYMBOLS OF DISTILLATION.

(*From Baker's " Jewell of Health,"* 1576.)

fighting shy of it. In housewifery there can be but little pretence, for no ignorance may remain hid. Bluff and a ready tongue or pen go a long way towards creating many a "brilliant reputation" in the "artistic" and vapid world which lives at clubs and restaurants, and runs societies for improving other people. But no bluff will ever avail in the presence of the food or drink in the preparation of which our skill has been employed. The products of housewifery speak for themselves; they are no empty expressions of sentiments which may be false or true.

In no way, indeed, can affection be displayed with more subtle grace and delicacy than by the thoughtfulness of the housewife. The greatest of poets has no such instrument at his command. Not that women, in order to be efficient in their homes, need be ignorant of the events and thoughts which are in progress outside. Quite otherwise, they should be able to be the boon companions of men. But what I would urge is that they should take over as their share of the necessary work of mankind the management of that department which is immediately associated with domestic life. In this there is nothing degrading. For, after all, it is housewifery to which nearly all the arts and sciences bring their secrets. Home and comfort, food and drink—it will be a long time before we can get quite away from the need of these things. To introduce science and order into the domestic

ALCHEMIST IN HIS LABORATORY.

(*From Baker's "Jewell of Health," 1576.*)

kingdom is a task worthy of the finest intellect; and that woman who by the use of brains organizes and systematizes her household work is she who can best front with a smiling face the difficulty of obtaining servants—which appears to be the great omnipresent trouble of Englishwomen.

In his summary of the "inward and outward vertues which ought to be in a compleate woman," Gervase Markham laid it down that she must be " of chast thought, stout courage, patient, untyred, watchfull, diligent, witty, pleasant, constant in friendship, full of good Neighbourhood, wise in discourse, but not frequent therein, sharpe and quicke of speech, but not bitter or talkative, secret in affaires, comfortable in her counsels, and generally skilfull in the worthy knowledges which doe belong to her Vocation." Later he says that, of all these " outward and active knowledges," " the first and most principall is a perfect skill and knowledge in Cookery, together with all the secrets belonging to the same, because it is a duty rarely belonging to a woman ; and shee that is utterly ignorant therein, may not by the Lawes of strict Justice challenge the freedome of marriage, because indeede shee can then but performe halfe her vow; for she may love and obey, but shee cannot cherish, serve, and keepe him with that true duty which is ever expected." The work that is most personal and nearest to our hand may be the most important and most valuable after all. It may also, as has been

ALCHEMIST PERFORMING MYSTIC RITES.

(*From Baker's "Jewell of Health," 1576.*)

said, be the finest and most dignified if we approach it in the right spirit.

The chipping away of the gross and unessential, with the consequent liberation of the true and fine, is as noble a process in cookery as in sculpture. Yet how different is the attitude of even the humblest artist in words or marble or paint towards his material and his work from that of the average housewife towards the flavours and fragrances which she is privileged to elucidate and to blend. It is a ludicrous thing that women cry out for spheres in which to display their power. And all these centuries they have been entrusted with the practice of an art with almost boundless possibilities, yet scarcely any of them have proved capable of rising above the status of artisans in that craft. Equally, one looks in vain for the Roger Bacons, the Harveys, the Darwins, or the Hubers of the kitchen. The processes of cooking do not seem to inspire women with any of the wonder, religion, and scientific zeal such as almost every branch of labour has inspired in man. Mechanically and brainlessly the recipes of the cookery books are followed by myriads of women everywhere, so that the compounding of foods and drinks is usually as uninteresting a piece of drudgery as can be conceived. One may well pray for a reaction, if indeed the art of house-wifery is not past praying for.

A S a volume of the present series will be devoted to the subject of The Dairy, which is too large a subject to be treated usefully in a single chapter, I shall here merely record such facts and formulæ as may be of help to those who have a general knowledge of dairy work, and also offer a little advice of a practical kind to those who have to deal with dairying on the smallest scale. A larder or store-room should never be used for the storage of milk, as the conditions required are somewhat different, and also because, more than almost any other substance, milk absorbs and is spoilt by any strong smell such as many stores yield to the air about them. The milk-room should be cool, only moderately light, well ventilated and somewhat dry, and should, if possible, face the east or north. There must be no possibility of gas from drain or manure heap coming into contact with the milk at any stage, either in milking-yard or dairy. The floor should be of tiles or concrete, and the shelves should be of slate or stone. The room and all vessels used should be kept scrupulously clean. If a separator is used, the milk should be put through the machine as soon as possible after milking, as the milk should have a temperature of about 90° F. If the cream is to be separated by " setting," the milk should be taken straight to the dairy as soon as possible after milking, and poured through a hair sieve or other strainer into shallow pans—about

DIAPHRAGM CHURN.

four to six inches deep. These should be kept at a temperature of between 46° and 56° F. In from twenty-four to thirty-six hours, according to the season (more quickly in summer), the cream is

THE MELOTTE CREAM SEPARATOR

separated by a flat perforated skimmer, or the milk is drawn off by a syphon, or by the removal of a plug. If skimmed, the process is repeated twelve hours later, and occasionally a third time after a similar period has elapsed. If clotted cream be desired, the pans—about six to eight inches deep—of milk, having stood in the dairy for twenty-four

A SMALL BUTTER-WORKER.

hours, are heated over a furnace or in a water-bath to a temperature of 175° F., and then again restored to the dairy to cool. The cream is then skimmed off the milk by means of the skimmer. If the cream is to be made into butter, it must be "ripened," but must not be allowed to become too sour. In summer, it must not be kept for more than two

days, and in winter for not more than four days.
It should be placed, as soon as separated, in an
earthenware cream-holder, large enough to hold
the entire cream to be used at a single churning.
When adding the cream from subsequent skimmings,
thoroughly stir the whole together. Keep the
cream cool until twenty-four hours before churning,
and add no fresh cream to the mixture within
twelve hours of the churning in summer, or within
twenty-four hours in winter. For the twenty-four
hours previous to churning, the cream must be kept
at a temperature of about 60° F. In summer, churn
at a temperature of from 57° to 59° F., and in
winter at from 59° to 63° F. The room, the
churn, and the cream should all be of about the
same temperature. The cream should be strained
through straining muslin into the churn, and the
latter should be not more than half full. Churn
rather slowly for the first five minutes, and allow
the gas to escape frequently, until no air rushes out
when the vent is opened. Directly you hear the
butter form or "break," open the churn and see
that it has come. It will resemble mustard seed.
Add for each gallon of cream a quart of cold water,
and slowly turn the churn for about half a minute.
Draw off the butter-milk, add to the butter the
same quantity of cold water as there was originally
of cream, give the churn a few turns quickly, and
then draw off the water. Repeat this process until
the water comes away quite clear. Then take the

butter out of the churn, place it on the worker, allow it to drain for quarter of an hour, and then work the whole mass together. Weigh it, and dredge over it from a quarter to three-quarters of an ounce of fine pure salt to the pound of butter, rolling it out and sprinkling the salt evenly and by degrees. Well roll it so as to mix the salt uniformly, and get rid of all the water, but do not

MILK-STRAINER FOR USE WITH MUSLIN.

DOUBLE PAN FOR DEVONSHIRE CREAM-RAISING.

overwork it. Place the butter in a cool place for six hours to harden before being made up. The hands should never touch the milk, cream, or butter at any stage; a thermometer should be used to measure the various temperatures of which knowledge is required; and the churn, worker, wooden hands, and other appliances should be prepared for use by first rinsing them with cold water, then scalding them with boiling water, rubbing them thoroughly with salt, and lastly rinsing them again with cold water.—*H. R.*

To pot Butter.—The great secret in potting butter so that it will keep is to extract from it every

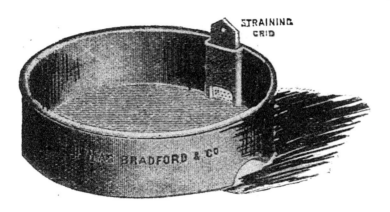

A SELF-SKIMMING PORCELAIN MILK-PAN.

drop of superfluous milk. This should be done either by working the butter thoroughly with a pair of the wooden " hands," or spatulas, used in all good dairies instead of the human hand, or by immersing

BUTTER-SCOOP.

the butter in hot water. In the latter case the milk will fall to the bottom, leaving the butter floating on the surface of the water. The butter should be packed in layers in an earthenware jar or crock, a little salt being sprinkled upon each layer. If this process is carefully carried out the butter will keep well. Another method is to make a pickle by pouring a quart of boiling water upon two pounds of salt, two ounces of loaf sugar, and one ounce of saltpetre. Let this stand till perfectly cold. Then put the butter into a jar, and keep it well covered with the pickle. Butter thus treated will keep sweet and firm throughout the hottest summer.

Cream Curds.—To one quart of new milk add four eggs, beaten together, and a little salt. Put it in a covered earthenware jar, and set it in a pan of water over the fire. Do not stir it, but as soon as the milk cracks, lay it upon a sieve to drain. Put it upon a china dish in large spoonfuls.—*J. R.*

CHEESE

I T is quite impossible here to give more than the merest outline of the steps taken in preparing the various sorts of cheese manufactured in this country. The processes will, moreover, be more fully described in a future volume of this series. Meanwhile, the reader may be advised to study the three pamphlets issued by the Royal Agricultural Society dealing with the practices of making Cheddar, Cheshire, and Stilton cheeses respectively. A brief summary may, however, be useful to those who can supplement this by a few actual observations of practical cheese-making by skilful operators.

In some ways, and by many connoisseurs, Stilton is considered the finest of English cheeses. The first step in its manufacture is the addition of Hansen's (or other) rennet, at the rate of one drachm to four gallons, to the fresh-strained milk when the milk has a temperature of from 80° to 85° F., the making-room being kept at a temperature of about 60° F. The whole is well stirred in a vat for eight minutes. When, in an hour so, the milk has completely turned, and the curd is ready for cutting and ladling, straining cloths, from thirty-six to forty-five inches square, are placed in earthenware curd-sinks, rods being used to support the sides. The curd is then ladled out of the vat by means of a half-gallon ladle, and about three gallons of curd are placed in each straining cloth, the plugs of the curd-sinks being in position. When the curd has stood for an hour and a half, open the plugs, drain off the whey, replace the plugs, tie the straining cloths, and tighten them every two hours until night, drawing off the whey each time. Then empty the curd on to the curd-tray, and leave it all night. On the next morning draw off the whey, cut the curd into three-inch cubes, and leave it to drain for a couple of hours. The milk from the next milking is treated in like manner. On the afternoon of the second day the two curds are thoroughly mixed together, broken up to the size of large filberts, salted at the rate of an ounce to three and a half pounds of curd, and placed into cheese hoops placed on round pieces of wood covered with "cheese greys." The hoops are put on the drainer, and turned every two hours during the first day by means of loose calico-covered discs over their top surfaces, similar to those which served as their basis. The temperature of the room whilst draining is going on must be about five degrees higher than that of the making-room. After the first day the cheeses are turned three times daily. In about a week the cheese can stand alone, and should be removed from the hoops, calico binders taking their place. The cheeses are still to be kept on the draining shelves, fresh binders being applied daily ; the outside of the cheese being gently scraped with a table knife at each binding. As soon as a dry crust begins to form, the binders are to be removed. The cheeses are to be kept at a temperature of about 55° F., and given plenty of air. They require turning daily. In about a month the cheeses are to be placed in a dark store-room having a temperature of 60° to 65° F., and are to be turned and brushed daily. In about six months they are fit for the table.

In making Cheddar cheese, the night's milk is placed in a vat, and left until the following morning, being kept fairly cool. If much cream has risen by the morning, this must be skimmed off, added to the morning's milk, and well stirred. The morning's milk must then be heated by the pan being placed in a vessel containing hot water until its temperature is raised to a point not far short of, but never exceeding, 95° F. The evening's milk is then added to it, and the joint temperature brought to about 80° to 85° F. Rennet is added, as in the case of Stilton cheese. In about an hour, when the curd breaks readily and clearly, as if cut, the curd is to be cut by a long thin knife into two-inch cubes. In about five minutes the curd is to be further broken up for about fifty minutes by the "breaker" until the pieces are of the size of peas, the whey keeping green all the while. Allow the whey to drain and separate for five or ten minutes, when it should be partly baled or syphoned off, heated to 130° F., and returned so as to raise the total temperature to 90° to

95° F., the curd being well stirred during the return of the heated whey, which process should be gradual, extending over ten minutes or more. The whey should now rest above the hard and shotty curd, which sinks to the bottom of the vat. In about a quarter of an hour the whey is drawn off, the curd is cut up, and the pieces are piled in a mound. Keep it warm by covering it with cloths, and in a quarter of an hour again cut it into pieces, turn it, and arrange it afresh in a mound. It is again covered for half an hour, then removed to a cooler, cut into small pieces, and covered for another half an hour. This is often again and again repeated until the curd is ripe for grinding. The curd having been ground, pure salt at the rate of an ounce to three pounds should be carefully dredged over, and mixed into it. The curd should then be placed in the cloth-lined moulds, and subjected to the press for twelve hours. The cloth is then changed, the cheese turned, and again pressed for twenty-four hours. This is repeated for four days, when the cheese is finally removed from the mould, bandaged after the manner of Stilton, and kept in a temperature of 65° to 70° F. for six weeks, being turned daily the while, and then in a temperature of 60° to 65° F., when it is turned on alternate days for another six or eight weeks.

Cream Cheese.—There are several soft cheeses well worth the attention of the small dairy owner. Simple cream cheese is the easiest of all, for one has only to take a quart of thick cream, put it with two drops of rennet into a napkin which has been freshly rinsed out in cold spring water, and sprinkle a little salt over it. Tie up the cream in the napkin as tightly as possible, and hang it up in the dairy. It may be eaten in twenty-four hours. The napkin must be changed at night, and again in the morning, for a fresh one wrung out in cold water. When the cream cheese comes out of the dining-room, it must be again tied up in a clean damp napkin and taken immediately to the dairy.

Grewelthorp Cream Cheese is equally simple in its manufacture. Take one quart of new milk, and put it with a few drops of rennet in a warm place, where it must remain for twenty-four hours. Then put in a little salt, stir the milk well, tie it up in a cloth, and hang it up in the dairy to drain. If a richer cheese is required, add half a pint of cream to the new milk.

A number of soft cheeses may be made with the help of some tinned iron cylindrical moulds open at both ends. These moulds may be of various diameters and depths. Some loose squares of wood, some entire and others perforated, of various sizes, to serve as bottoms and tops of the moulds, must also be provided; and straw mats of the same size as the boards are also desirable. A good average size for the moulds is five inches in diameter, and four inches in depth. About two quarts of milk are required to make one cheese for this size mould.

To make Camembert, the rennet diluted with water is added to milk of a temperature of about 85° F., and the whole is stirred for three minutes. It is then covered for about four hours, until no curd adheres to the finger when placed on its surface. The curd is then ladled in slices into the moulds, each mould being placed on a straw mat, with a board below, resting on a sloping table. The full moulds are allowed to drain for about six hours in a temperature of 60° F. A clean mat and board are then placed at the top of the mould, the latter inverted, and the previous base removed and cleaned. Repeat this changing and inversing twice a day for two days. Then remove the cheeses from the moulds, sprinkle some salt on top and bottom, and stand them on straw or straw-mats in a temperature of about 50° to 55° F., a free current of air being carried through the drying-room. The cheeses require turning each morning and evening for another three days, then every morning for a week, and afterwards on alternate days. In about a fortnight, when the cheeses cease to stick to the hand when touched, they are put in a cool (about 50° F.), dark, slightly damp cellar to ripen for about another fortnight, being turned on alternate days.

Gervais Cheese.—Messrs. Long and Morton, in their book "The Dairy," give directions for preparing a Mignon or Gervais. This cheese is made of a mixture of cream and milk set at a temperature of 65° F. Six drops of Hansen's rennet are sufficient for two and a half quarts of milk and one quart of cream. The curd is fit to cut in from six to eight hours, when it is removed into a cloth, in which it is allowed to drain until it is sufficiently solid and consistent to press.

Removed into a clean cloth, it is laid within a wooden frame with open sides, and pressed with a close-fitting follower of wood, heavy enough to cause the whey to drain away without any loss of cream. This pressure, with one or two manipulations, with the object of maintaining evenness of consistence, continues until the curd is as thick as an ice cream, when it is pressed into specially made paper-lined moulds. It may be eaten about three days later.

To pot Cheese.—A pleasant form of potted food is made by pounding together in a mortar a pound of cheese, three ounces of quite fresh butter, and half a table-spoonful each of castor sugar and made mustard. This mixture should be packed in jars, covered with clarified butter, and securely covered. It should not be kept longer than a fortnight.

PICKLING MEAT

IN pickling or salting meat, it is better to let the fresh joint first hang for two or three days untouched. This will make the meat more tender. Before salting it, be careful to remove every pipe or kernel in the meat, and fill up all holes with salt. Do not attempt to pickle meat in very cold frosty weather, or in warm damp weather. It is a good plan to sprinkle the meat with water and then to hang it up for a few hours before salting it : this cleanses it from any blood, and makes the flavour more delicate.

A good brine, sufficient for twenty pounds of beef, is made by mixing together three pounds of salt, three-quarters of a pound of sugar, and two ounces of saltpetre. Boil these ingredients together for twenty minutes in two gallons of water, skimming off all scum. Let the liquid get quite cold before you pour it over the meat, and see that the joint is thoroughly covered with the brine. For a smaller piece of meat the quantities given for the brine can be easily reduced, following the same proportions carefully. The meat must be turned over every day, and well basted with the brine ; and the salting pan or tub must be covered with a clean piece of tamis-cloth, or other porous woollen material. The meat will be ready for use in a fortnight.

In cooking pickled or salted meat, two things must be recollected. First, that, in order to make salted meat tender, it must be put into cold water when first placed on the fire. Secondly, that it is next to impossible to cook salted meat too slowly.

Spiced Round of Beef.—Procure a round of beef weighing from thirty-five to forty pounds ; remove the bone, and lay the beef in a stone pan. Well rub into the meat all over (not omitting the sides of the round as well as the top and bottom) a mixture made of four pounds of salt, two pounds of coarse brown sugar, a quarter of a pound of saltpetre, and two ounces of *sal prunella* from the chemist. Turn the beef every day, and well rub into it the brine which it makes. Let it remain in pickle for one month. When ready for cooking, let the beef be closely bound into shape with coarse webbing. Lay it in a large kettle or pot, and cover the beef with broth as cold as it can be to remain liquid. Add plenty of rough vegetables, such as carrots, turnips, onions, and celery, all sliced. Dry in the oven a sufficient quantity of ginger, cloves, mace, and peppercorns to make two ounces of each when dried and pounded fine in a mortar. Add these to the beef. Bring the broth slowly to a very gentle boil, and then keep it simmering very gently for twelve hours, turning the beef over at the end of six hours. It must on no account be allowed to boil, or it will be hard and tasteless. Remove the kettle from the fire, but let the beef remain in it for two days, when it will have become perfectly cold and firm. Take off the webbing, and the beef will be ready for eating.

Welsh Beef—Rub two ounces of saltpetre into a round of beef; let it rest an hour, and then rub it with equal parts of pepper, salt, and allspice. Keep the beef in the brine which this will make for fifteen days, turning and rubbing it every day. Then put the beef into a large earthenware round pan, first coating the bottom of the pan with a layer of suet. Put another layer of suet over the top of the beef, and then cover the pan with a coarse paste of flour and water. Bake in a slow oven for eight hours, then pour off any gravy, and let the beef get cold before it is taken out of the pan.

To make Sausages.—Sausages are generally put into the thoroughly cleaned skins of the intestine of the pig. But they are sometimes preferred without this covering. Take two pounds of fresh pork, using both fat and lean in equal proportions, but avoiding the coarse fat from the inside of the pig. Mince the pork as finely as possible, and then pass it twice through the mincing machine. Blanch and mince two dessert-spoonfuls of sage, add four ounces of freshly made bread-crumbs, and season with pepper and a dust of salt. Mix all thoroughly together, and keep the sausage-meat in a cool place. When wanted do not use skins, but form the sausage-meat into small round cakes three-quarters of an inch thick, flour them, and fry them in butter from ten to fifteen minutes, turning them often.

To cook Sausages.—This recipe is for sausages which have been put into skins by the sausage machine. Plenty of time must be allowed for cooking the sausages, for if they are done too quickly the skins will burst. About ten minutes is enough over a low fire, the skins having been well pricked over first. The sausages are much better if they are first pricked, then put into hot water and brought slowly to the boil, simmered for five minutes, drained, and finally fried in bacon fat till they are brown. Serve round a pile of mashed potato, or shape the mashed potato into long ovals, fake them on a buttered baking-tin, and when very hot, lay the potato ovals on a hot dish, and put a sausage on each.

Ham.—Tastes vary much as to the best size of a ham ; some people like a York ham weighing thirty or forty pounds, others prefer a foreign ham not exceeding a few pounds in weight. Monsieur de St. Simon, writing in 1721, said he could never forget the delicious flavour of the little Spanish hams he had once tasted near Burgos. The pigs which furnished these hams lived on the flesh of vipers, and in our own day the hams of the little black pigs of North Carolina, which feed on rattle-snakes, are esteemed an especial delicacy. The peculiar flavour of a Westphalian ham is due to the smoke of a fire of juniper branches over which the ham is hung for three weeks.

It was formerly the custom to put a thick coat of mortar over the inside of a cured ham to keep out the air, and to prevent the mildew, or "rust," which damp is sure to cause. A better way is to cover the underneath portion of the ham (where the knife has been used), and also the knuckle-end of the bone, with a paste made of flour and water. This paste entirely prevents any "rusting," or, in other words, the minute fungus caused by damp.

To cure a Ham weighing from fifteen to eighteen pounds. Norfolk Recipe.—One pound of treacle, half a pound of coarse brown sugar, half a pound of bay-salt (*i.e.* sea-salt), one pound of common salt, one ounce of saltpetre, and two ounces of *sal prunella* (*i.e.* saltpetre which has been fused, and is sold by chemists). Pound all these together as finely as possible, and rub the ham thoroughly with them. Lay the ham in a tub, covered with the pickle, and let it remain there for a month. It must be turned and basted with the pickle every other day. When taken out of the pickle, let the ham dry for a day or two, standing on end. Then brush it over with Crosse and Blackwell's essence of smoke. This preparation gives to the ham all the flavour of the chimney-smoke in which hams used to be hung. [This recipe was given to me by a friend in whose family it has been used year by year during four generations.]

Pickle for Bacon.—Weigh each flitch, and allow for every stone (a stone of meat weighs eight pounds) one pound of salt, two ounces of bay-salt, two ounces of saltpetre, and three ounces of coarse brown sugar. Sprinkle the flitches with salt, and drain them for twenty-four hours. Mix the salt, bay-salt, saltpetre, and sugar thoroughly together, and rub all well into the flitches, rubbing the ends as well as the sides. Do this every day for a month. Then hang up the flitches to dry, sewing a bag of coarse muslin over each. [Do not use paper, as it breaks in damp weather. Muslin is a far better protector from the flies, which are always more partial to salt meat than to any other.] The flitch, from the Old English word, is one side of the pig.

To cure Pig's Cheeks.—Do not use any saltpetre, but clear the two cheeks well, take out the bones, rub well with common salt, let the cheeks drain, and next day rub them again with salt, using a fresh supply. Then mix four ounces of salt with five ounces of coarse brown sugar, cover the cheeks with this mixture, and turn them every day. They will be sufficiently cured in twelve days. If saltpetre is used the cheeks will be hard.

To boil a Ham.—The great point in boiling a ham is to boil it as slowly as possible. If a ham is small and rather fresh, it will need soaking in cold water for only eighteen hours before it is boiled ; but as a rule a ham should be soaked for forty-eight hours, the water being changed three or even four times during that period. After the ham has been soaked, scrub it well with a dry, stiff brush, so as to remove all smoke and discoloration from the surface. Trim off any ragged or untidy parts, reserving them for the stock-pot. Now put the ham into a ham-kettle or a large pan, and cover it completely with cold water to the depth of one inch. Let the water heat as slowly as possible, so that it may be an hour and a half or two hours before it comes to the boil. It is a good rule to allow twenty-five minutes' simmering to each pound of ham. Skim off all scum as it rises. When the liquor is perfectly clear put in one shallot, a stick of celery, two turnips, two or three onions, and three carrots, also add (in a muslin bag) a bunch of parsley, a sprig of thyme and of marjoram, some chopped lemon-peel, and twelve peppercorns. Cover the pan closely, reduce the heat under it, and let the ham simmer very gently for five hours. At the end of that time lift the ham out, peel off the outside skin, and trim it a little if this is needed. Brush the ham over with thin glaze, or cover it with raspings of bread, and set it in a slow oven to brown.

To steam a Ham.—If the ham is quite small this is an excellent way of cooking it. As soon as the ham has been soaked, scrubbed, and trimmed, put it into the steamer over boiling water. Allow twenty-five minutes to every pound of ham, and keep the water under the steamer boiling hard. Either glaze the ham or cover with raspings.

To pot Pounded Meat, Chicken, or Fish.—Cook
the meat until it is very tender and easily separated
from the bones. Mince it, and then pound it with
a quarter of its weight of clarified butter, together
with pepper and such other spices and herbs as are
liked. Then fill the pots with the mixture, press
it tightly, and cover with clarified butter.

*T*O *smoke Fish.*—Having opened and cleaned the fish, place them in salt and saltpetre, eight parts to one, and leave them over the night. Then wipe them, and hang them in a row, by a stout wire passed through their eyes, over a sawdust fire for about twenty-four hours.

To salt Fish.—Having opened and cleaned the fish, place them in strong brine for twenty hours. Drain them and place them in jars, with layers of salt between the several layers of fish. Securely cover the jars until the fish are wanted. Soak the fish for four hours in lukewarm water and dry before cooking.

To pickle Fish.—Having opened and cleaned the fish and removed their heads, place them in a jar for twenty-four hours with layers of salt between the several layers of fish. Drain them, and boil them for two minutes with vinegar, onions, cloves, peppercorns, and bay .leaves. Place them in jars, pour the liquid over them, and closely fasten down the covers.

To pot Shrimps.—Boil some shrimps, and as soon as cold remove their shells. Mix with them a little mace, cayenne, salt, and pepper, and pack them tightly in the pots. Bake for about ten minutes in a slow oven, and when cold pour over them a quarter of an inch thickness of melted butter which is just beginning to set.

EGGS

*T*O *preserve Eggs.*—Gather them quite fresh, thoroughly clean them, and place them in a covered vessel containing a 10 per cent. solution of sodium silicate (soluble glass). Eggs thus treated keep perfectly fresh for six months, or even longer.

FOR pickling, the fruit, or leaves, or bulbs should be in perfect condition and thoroughly cleaned. Strong vinegar of good quality should be used, and the spices should be fresh and good. The mixing and heating of the vinegar is best performed in unglazed stoneware vessels ; if these are unavailable, enamelled iron pans should be used. Pickling consists in preserving fruits or other vegetable products in spiced vinegar, the details of the process differing slightly according to the product to be pickled. To make the spiced vinegar, place in a stoneware or enamelled boiling-pan a quart of strong vinegar, from half an ounce to four ounces of black peppercorns, a couple of ounces of crushed ginger, and from two to eight ounces of mustard seed. Boil this mixture for four minutes. If liked, any or all of the following spices may be added to, and boiled with, the vinegar, in addition to those just named : from one to four blades of mace, from two to ten cloves, from four to eight allspice, and from two to eight grains of cayenne pepper.

Implements.—Unglazed stone jars are of all vessels the most suitable for the containing of pickles, both by virtue of their chemical composition, and on account of their pleasant wholesome look. Glass bottles are next best for the purpose. In any case, the great thing to be remembered is that no metallic substance must be allowed to come into contact with the pickle or with the vinegar which is to be used. Wooden spoons alone should be used for mixing. For closing the mouths of the jars or bottles, corks should be employed, and further security from contact with the air should be ensured by covering the corked mouths with tinfoil, bladder, or parchment-paper. It is desirable that the vessels be furnished with mouths of smaller size than is usually the case, as the larger the mouth the greater the risk of contamination by exposure to the air.

To pickle Red Cabbage.—Cut the cabbages into shreds, place them in a large jar with plenty of salt well intermingled. Leave them alone for two days, then pour off the liquid, dry the cabbage for a few hours in the air, pack it in the pickling jars to about an inch from the opening, and pour sufficient cold spiced vinegar to fill each jar completely, interspersing some of the spices among the cabbage. Cork and seal at once.

To pickle Shallots.—Peel the shallots, and place them in a large jar with plenty of salt well intermingled. In two days pour off the liquid, and dry the shallots in the air for a few hours. Then pack them in the pickling jars, and pour boiling spiced vinegar to fill each jar completely, interspersing some of the spices among the shallots. Cork and seal whilst hot. If the vinegar be poured off in a

OLD DISTILLING FURNACES AND STILLS.

(From the title page of the first volume of Brunschwig's
"Liber de Arte Distillandi," 1500.)

week, reboiled, and returned to the jars, the pickle will keep much longer.

To pickle Walnuts.—Take walnuts gathered about July, when still young and soft enough to be pierced by a pin, and place them in a large jar, with plenty of salt well interspersed and covering. In eight days pour off the liquid, and wipe and then dry the nuts in the air for a few hours. Pierce each walnut with a stout needle, place them in the pickling jars, and pour boiling spiced vinegar on them so as to fill the jars. Cover with corks, and each week for three weeks pour off the vinegar, reboil it, and fill up the jars with boiling spiced vinegar. Then finally cork and seal.

To pickle Gherkins.—Place the gherkins in a large jar with plenty of salt over and among them. In six days pour off the liquid and add a little water to it, so that it may be a brine strong enough that an egg will float thereon. Boil this liquid and pour it over the gherkins. In twenty-four hours pour off the liquid, wipe and dry the gherkins in the air, place them in the pickling jars, and fill the latter with boiling spiced vinegar. Cork and seal. If the vinegar be poured off in a week, reboiled, and again placed in the jars, the pickle will keep much longer.

To make a Green Tomato Pickle.—Take a gallon of green tomatoes and a quart of onions ; slice them and cover them with salt. In twenty-four hours pour off the liquid, and slowly boil for about an hour the tomatoes and onions in a quart of spiced vinegar, to which a pound of sugar and a tea-spoonful of celery seed have been added. When tender, take the mixture off the fire, bottle, cork, and seal.

To make a Ripe Tomato Pickle.—Substitute ripe tomatoes for the tomatoes and onions in the last recipe. Halve the quantity of vinegar, and omit the celery seed.

To pickle Plums.—Prick four pounds of plums and place them in a fire-proof stoneware pan with two and a half pounds of sugar. Carefully bring to the boil, and add two-thirds of a pint of spiced vinegar. Boil for a few minutes, take out the plums, cool them, and place them in the pickle-jars. Boil up the liquid again, and pour it whilst boiling over the plums so as to fill the jars. Cork and seal at once.

To pickle Samphire.—Gather samphire whilst it is green, about August, break it into sprigs, place in a jar, and add abundance of salt over and amongst the sprigs. In two days pour off the liquid, and dry the samphire for a few hours in the air. Pack it in jars, pour boiling unspiced vinegar over it so as to fill the jars, and boil in the oven until the samphire is green and crisp, and at once remove. Cork and seal.

To make Nasturtium Pickle.—Place some green nasturtium seeds in a weak solution of salt for three days. Then soak them in cold water for twelve hours. Strain and place them in small jars, and pour boiling vinegar over them.

Some other Pickles.—Young pea pods, young French bean pods, cauliflower, unripe gooseberries, and umbels of elderberry flowers gathered before they expand, barberries (Mrs. Glasse recommends that a little sprig of boiled fennel be placed at the top of each jar before sealing), and sliced boiled beet-root, are pickled as directed for red cabbage.

Unripe, but fully grown radish pods, are pickled as directed for gherkins.

Onions and young mushrooms (which should be rubbed with salt but not peeled) are pickled as directed for shallots.

Small apples, pears, peaches, apricots, and damsons may be used to make sweet pickles as directed for plums. But apples, pears, peaches, and apricots require to be peeled before being pickled.

To make Sauerkraut.—Take a dozen fine, hard-hearted, white cabbages, remove the outer leaves, and shred the hearts into small shreds. Place these shreds into a large tub, and over each layer sprinkle a little salt (about six pounds in all). Press the layers of cabbage firmly down, and, when the tub is full, sprinkle salt over the top of the heap of cabbage. On this place a piece of linen, and a wooden cover on the linen. Weigh down the cover by means of a large stone or other weight. The cover must accurately fit the tub, and slide down within the staves. The tub should then be placed in a warm room till fermentation has begun. Wash and replace the linen cover every fortnight. In three weeks the sauerkraut will be fit for use, though it will keep good for more than a year.

MUSTARD.—The simplicity of its manufacture probably accounts for our persistence in serving in our mustard-pots the never-varying paste of mustard and water. Yet the infinite variety of flavours which may be introduced into our table mustards should sufficiently reward us for the little trouble entailed in mixing them. As all these made mustards contain spices or herbs which lose much of their aroma by exposure to the air, they should be put into jars and securely corked directly they are made. Ordinary mustard also soon loses its piquancy if left exposed to the air. It should therefore be kept in a properly closed bottle or jar. It is best to make small quantities of ordinary mustard frequently, almost daily, as required.

To make Ordinary Mustard.—Take a bare table-spoonful of mustard, white and brown in equal parts, and mix therewith one tea-spoonful of salt, adding to the mixture, little by little, two table-spoonfuls of cold water, stirring the while. Continue stirring for a few minutes.

Mustard with Horseradish.—Boil a table-spoonful of grated horseradish in half a tea-cupful of water for ten minutes, and allow to get cold. Then mix the mustard as in the last recipe, adding the horse-radish and two table-spoonfuls of the water in which it has been boiled instead of the plain water.

To make a simple French Mustard.—Proceed as in the last recipe, except that a minced shallot should be substituted for the horseradish, and that only the water, having been cleared by straining, is added to the mustard-flour. A tea-spoonful of good vinegar is to be added to the mixture and thoroughly incorporated.

To make a Spiced Mustard (Recipe 1).—Take a quarter of a pound of mustard-flour, pour over it three small tea-cupfuls of boiling vinegar, keep the mixture just below boiling-heat for about forty-five minutes, add a salt-spoonful of ground ginger, half a salt-spoonful of powdered cloves, and a salt-spoonful of grated nutmeg, and heat for five minutes longer.

To make a Spiced Mustard (Recipe 2).—Take a tumblerful of vinegar, and place therein two salt-spoonfuls of salt, a salt-spoonful of scraped horse-radish, and half a salt-spoonful of powdered cloves. At the end of three days strain off the liquid and add a sufficiency of mustard-flour—about three ounces—to make a thick paste.

To make a Spiced Mustard (Recipe 3).—Mix together a tea-spoonful each of powdered mace, ground black pepper, powdered dill seeds, and powdered cinnamon, a slightly smaller quantity of powdered cloves, a table-spoonful of powdered tarragon leaves, and three pints of vinegar. Heat for an hour, strain, and then mix with about a pound of mustard-flour and a quarter of a pound of castor sugar to make a thick paste.

To make Frankfort Mustard.—Mix together a quarter of a pound of castor sugar, an ounce of allspice, half an ounce of powdered cloves, and a pound of ground mustard—white and brown, in equal parts. Mix into a thick paste with wine vinegar.

To make Jesuits' Mustard.—Thoroughly mix ten sardines, a quarter of a pound of ground brown mustard, three-quarters of a pound of ground white mustard, and two hundred capers. Make into a paste with about a quart of boiling vinegar.

To make Mustard as at Düsseldorf.—Take two earthenware pans, and place in each a quart of vinegar. In one place a quarter of an ounce of thyme leaves, and in the other place three minced onions. Let them stand for forty-eight hours. Bruise half a pound of white mustard seed and half a pound of black mustard seed, and put them in a pan with a tea-spoonful of powdered cloves, a tea-spoonful of powdered coriander, half a pound of salt, and the strained vinegar. Thoroughly mix. Add a little more vinegar if the mixture is too thick, or a little more mustard if it is too thin. Parsley, celery, or other herbs may be used instead of onions to flavour the vinegar.

To make an Aromatic Mustard Powder.—In making a mixed powder of this kind, it is absolutely essential to success that each of the articles be thoroughly dry previous to being mixed. A good result is obtained by mixing a quarter of a

DISTILLING OYLE OUT OF SEEDES.

(*From Baker's "Jewell of Health,"* 1576.)

pound of salt, a pound of mustard, half an ounce each of dried garlic, dried thyme, dried tarragon, and mixed spices—all finely powdered. The mixture should be stored in air-tight boxes or bottles.

To make a Spiced Table Vinegar.—Mix in an earthenware pan two ounces of cloves, a quarter of an ounce of mace, and the same quantity each of orange blossoms and cassia bark. Pour a quart of heated strong vinegar over the spices, and let the mixture digest in a warm place for a week. Strain, filter through filter-paper, and bottle.

To make an Aromatic Table Vinegar (Recipe 1).—Chop up one ounce each of bay leaves, leaves of rosemary, and leaves of sage, and place them in a fireproof earthenware pan; add thereto a quarter of an ounce each of cloves, zedoary root, and chillis. Pour on the mixture a quart of heated strong vinegar, and let it digest in a warm place for a week. Strain, filter, and bottle.

To make an Aromatic Table Vinegar (Recipe 2).—Chop up one ounce each of thyme leaves, basil leaves, leaves of marjoram, leaves of tarragon, and bean leaves. Add thereto half an ounce each of chopped shallots and celery. Pour on the mixture a quart of heated strong vinegar, and treat as in the last recipe.

To make an Aromatic Table Vinegar (Recipe 3).—Chop up and mix half a pound of tarragon leaves, and a quarter of a pound each of rocambole, shallots, anchovies, capers, and bay leaves. Pour over them three quarts of heated strong vinegar, and treat as in the first recipe.

To make Aromatic Table Vinegar (Recipe 4).— The leaves of any sweet herb, having been dried, may be lightly placed—not pressed—in a bottle till it is full, and vinegar poured over them and allowed to stand for six weeks. It may then be strained off and bottled.

To make Aromatic Wines.—The leaves of any sweet herb are to be treated as above, but sherry is to take the place of the vinegar.

To make Curry Powder.—Pound to a fine powder and mix thoroughly together a quarter of a pound each of coriander seed and turmeric, an ounce each of mustard, ginger, and black pepper, and half an ounce each of cardamom, cumin, and pimento.

To make Mushroom Catsup.—Wipe, but do not wash or skin, some freshly gathered, fully ripe mushrooms, and place them in a jar with layers of salt between the several layers of mushrooms and over the whole, allowing six ounces of salt to a gallon of mushrooms. Cover the jar loosely with a cloth, and place it in a warm room until the next day. Crush the mushrooms, place the whole in a cool oven for half an hour, and strain through coarse muslin. Boil the liquid with peppercorns, half an ounce to the quart; mace, a dram to the quart; cloves, a dozen to the quart; and bruised ginger, half an ounce to the quart. When the liquid has boiled down to a half, take it off the fire, allow it to cool, strain through very coarse straining cloth, and bottle in small, well-corked bottles. If these bottles are treated as the bottles of fruit in fruit-bottling are treated, the catsup will keep the better.

To make Tomato Catsup.—Boil a quart of perfectly ripe tomatoes with a table-spoonful of black pepper, a salt-spoonful of salt, a tea-spoonful each of ground cloves and allspice, and half a tea-spoonful of mustard in a pint of vinegar for three hours. Strain, and, when the mixture is cold, bottle and seal.

To make Walnut Catsup.—Boil a gross of soft, young walnuts, crushed, two ounces each of ground nutmeg and black pepper, half an ounce each of ground mace and ginger, and fifty cloves, ground, in two quarts of vinegar for forty minutes. Strain, and, when the mixture is cold, bottle and seal.

To make a Piquant Sauce (Recipe 1).—Boil half an ounce of cayenne, half an ounce of cochineal, half an ounce of mixed garlic, and half a dozen cloves in a quart of vinegar for twenty minutes. Strain, and, when the liquor is cool, add two ounces of essence of anchovies, half a pint of an equal mixture of walnut and mushroom catsup, and half a pint of good port. Thoroughly mix and bottle.

To make a Piquant Sauce (Recipe 2).—Boil a quarter of a pound of bruised cloves, a quarter of a pound of minced shallots, and half an ounce of cayenne pepper in half a gallon of vinegar for twenty minutes. Strain, and, when the liquor is cool, add half a pint of an equal mixture of walnut catsup and soy. Thoroughly mix and bottle.

To make a Piquant Sauce (*Receipe* 3).—Boil a quarter of a pound each of allspice, minced shallots, and minced garlic, and two ounces of salt in a quart of vinegar for twenty minutes. Strain, and, when the mixture is cool, add a gallon each of walnut catsup and mushroom catsup. Thoroughly mix and bottle.

To make Anchovy Sauce.—Heat, until it thickens, a mixture of a pint of vinegar, a pint and a quarter of water, two pounds and a half of butter, three-quarters of a pound of flour, and thirty minced anchovies. Rub the mixture through a coarse hair sieve and bottle.

To make a Salad Dressing to be stored.—Salad dressings should be mixed freshly as required; but it is sometimes thought desirable to keep a stock dressing bottled and ready for all emergencies. Thoroughly beat the yolks of three eggs, and gradually stir in half a tea-cupful of olive oil, together with a table-spoonful of mustard, a little pepper, two table-spoonfuls of salt, and half a tea-cupful of vinegar; adding, last of all, the well-beaten whites of the three eggs. Bottle in well-stoppered bottles.

PRESERVES

IT is easy to make good jam at home if a few simple rules are followed. Excellent jams can, it is true, be bought, but they are generally too sweet, a large proportion of sugar being used in order to make the jam keep for a considerable time.

Rule 1.—Use only fresh fruit which has been gathered in dry weather.

2. Allow three-quarters of a pound of sugar to one pound of all fruit, except stone fruit. Stone fruit requires an extra quarter of a pound of sugar. Break the sugar small, but do not pound it; if the sugar is pounded the syrup will not be clear. Use the best sugar, as the inferior kinds produce much more scum.

3. Never set the preserving-pan flat on the fire. If you do, the fruit will stick to it, and burn. Raise the pan on a trivet a little above the fire, and not exactly over the hottest part. Stir the jam with a wooden spoon all the time that the sugar and fruit are boiling together. An iron spoon ruins both the flavour and the colour of jam. Stir gently at first, more quickly as the boiling of the jam proceeds. Skim off all scum as it rises.

4. Put the fruit into the preserving-pan, sprinkle in some of the sugar, and as the fruit juices, add

the rest of the sugar by degress. When the sugar is all dissolved bring the jam to the boil.

5. Never boil jam longer than twenty minutes. If it is boiled too long the jam will be sticky, but if not boiled enough it will not keep. When the scum ceases to rise, put a few drops of the jam on a cold plate, watch it for a minute, and if it sets, and does not flow freely, the jam is done.

6. Warm the jam-pots before you pour the hot jam into them ; if you do not they may crack. Fill the pots to within half an inch of the top, and wipe off any drops spilt with a cloth wrung out in hot water. If this is not attended to, there will be great difficulty in scraping off the drops when the jam has cooled.

7. The day after the jam is made, and when it has become quite cold, lay a round of thin paper on the top of each pot. Then take a sufficient number of the vegetable parchment covers which are sold for tying over jam-pots, soak them for a minute or two in cold water, wipe them dry, stretch one over each pot, and tie it round with string. The parchment tightens as it dries, and excludes the air from the jam. When the covers are dry, write in ink on each the name of the jam and the date.

8. Always keep jam in a cool, dry place. Damp makes it mouldy, heat makes it ferment.

9. Never put one pot of jam exactly on the top of another, but set one row of pots on the edges

of the row beneath, leaving a clear space in the centre of each pot.

Different fruits require different treatment when made into jam. Thus, strawberries must be carefully stirred, raspberries must be mashed with a wooden spoon ; and both these fruits, being soft and juicy, require less boiling than the drier kinds. Dry fruits, such as apples, should always be put first into a covered jar set in a pan of boiling water, and kept there until they are thoroughly softened. Fruit, with the exception of the very juicy kinds, takes longer to boil than sugar, so that it is well to cook the fruit partially before adding the sugar. Over-boiled sugar spoils the texture of jam.

Rhubarb jam requires the addition of a little root-ginger and a few strips of lemon-peel.

Orange Marmalade.—Allow for every pound of oranges one pint of water and three-quarters of a pound of sugar.

Pare Seville oranges very thin, and boil the rind till tender. Boil it in plenty of water for about three-quarters of an hour. At the end of this time the orange rind should be so tender that a straw will pierce it. Then cut it into very thin strips about half an inch long. Take off the tough white coat of each orange, and throw it away. Then scrape out the pulp and juice very carefully, and throw the pips into cold water. When they have remained in the water for a short time, squeeze them through a cloth, and add a pint of the water in which the pips have been soaked to every three-quarters of a pound of the sugar. The reason for steeping the pips is that they yield a glutinous substance, which adds richness to the marmalade. Boil the syrup for twenty minutes, allowing three-quarters of a pound of sugar and one pint of water to every pound of orange pulp. Put the pulp and juice into the syrup, and boil for half an hour, carefully skimming off the scum as it rises. During the last five minutes add the shreds of orange-peel. Put the marmalade into pots, and tie them down next day.

Clear Orange Marmalade.—In this marmalade there are no shreds of orange-peel. Cut the oranges in half after they are peeled and freed from the white skin. Boil them for three-quarters of an hour, allowing one pint of water to twelve oranges. Strain off the juice, and boil it up sharp for ten minutes. Allow three-quarters of a pound of sugar to every pint of juice. Boil for twenty or five-and-twenty minutes till it jellies. Four oranges make a pound pot of marmalade. It is an improvement if half the peel taken from the oranges is grated finely, and boiled with the oranges.

Quince Marmalade.—Scald the quinces, pare, core, and quarter them. To four pounds of fruit add three pounds and a half of sugar. Take three pints of the water the quinces were scalded in, and boil in it both the parings and the cores. Strain the water, and add it to the quinces and the sugar. Let it stand all night. Next day set the quinces over a slow fire, and bring them very gradually to the boil, skimming and stirring them all the time they are cooking.

Crab-apples, Siberian crab-apples, and the fruit of the Pyrus Japonica, or Japanese quince, all make excellent preserve.

Crab-apple Marmalade.—Parboil the crab-apples, and pulp them through a sieve or colander. Pare six large common apples, boil them till quite soft, and pass them through the sieve, when they will yield all the liquid they contain. To every quart of crab-apple pulp add one gill of the liquid from the common apples ; and allow three-quarters of a pound of sugar to every pound of pulp. Boil all together for fifteen minutes, stirring the whole time.

Fruit Jellies.—In making fruit jellies only the clear juice extracted from the fruit is used. The fruit must be softened by being placed in a jar set in boiling water, after which the juice must be allowed to drip through a hair sieve or a piece of canvas. The fruit must on no account be squeezed or rubbed with the hand or spoon, but it may be pressed down by a plate with a weight set upon it. Boil the juice for ten minutes, weigh it, and when it boils up again, add half a pound of sugar to every pint of juice. Then boil the whole sharp for five or ten minutes more, skimming off all scum.

Clear Apple Jelly.—Pare and core half a peck of green apples, cut them up, and drop them as you cut them into two quarts of water. Pare two small lemons, cut them up, removing the pips, and add them to the apples, reserving the lemon-peel. Put the apple-parings and the cores with the apples, and boil all together very slowly till the fruit is quite a pulp. Then strain it through a jelly-bag, and to every pint of liquid add half a pound of lump sugar. Boil the whole very fast with the peel of the two lemons, skimming thoroughly all the time. It ought to jelly in three-quarters of an hour ; try it by dropping a few drops on a cold plate. When sufficiently done take out all the lemon-peel, and pour the jelly into moulds or small pots.

Cranberry Jelly can be made in this way from the Russian and Swedish cranberries now sold, but cranberries will require a pound of sugar to the pint of juice. Cranberries should not be boiled longer than twenty minutes.

Medlar Jelly.—Gather the medlars when quite sound, wipe them well, and let them stew in the preserving-pan with just enough boiling water to cover them till they are in a pulp. Drain the fruit through a piece of canvas, but do not press the pulp. Weigh the juice, and allow half a pound of sugar to every pint. Boil it till quite clear, stirring and skimming well. When it jellies, pour it into small moulds, and let it set.

Currant Jelly (*No.* 1).—Strip red currants from their stalks, and put them into the oven. When quite juicy, pass them through a hair sieve or a coarse cloth. To every pint of juice allow a pound of loaf sugar well beaten and sifted. Heat the sugar on a dish in the oven, putting it between two sheets of foolscap paper, and when the currant juice has boiled for a couple of minutes, strew the sugar into it by degrees whilst the juice is boiling hot. It will jelly immediately, and gain flavour by keeping. Put it at once into pots.

Currant Jelly (*No.* 2).—To six pounds of red, white, or black currants add four pounds of. sugar and half a pint of currant juice extracted from additional currants. Stir the fruit well together in a preserving-pan, set it on a brisk fire, and when it boils up, pass it through a cloth into a basin with a lip. Pour the jelly from the basin at once into pots. Let the pots remain uncovered for nine days, and then tie them up.

Blackberry Jelly.—Take six pounds of blackberries before they are quite ripe, pick them from the stalks, and put them into a jar. Tie the jar up closely, set it in a pan of water on the fire till the blackberries become pulp. Then strain the fruit through a cloth, and to one pint of juice add one pound of sifted sugar. Boil it to a jelly, and pour it into pots for use. Blackberry jelly is much improved if half the quantity of blackberries is used and the other half made up of bullaces or wild plums. But bullaces are now rare.

Scotch "Jam Jelly."—This preserve is made from the berries of the mountain ash, gathered when they have become nearly (but not quite) ripe.

Take off the stalks, and stew the berries in a jar set in boiling water. They take many hours' stewing before they become tender, but in the end they make excellent jelly. For the mountain-ash berries allow a pound of sugar to a pound of pulp.

Damson Cheese.—Stew the damsons till tender in a jar set in boiling water. Rub them through a coarse sieve to take off the skins. Take out the stones, crack them, and blanch the kernels. Boil the cheese for one hour. Then weigh it, and add one pound of sugar to two quarts of the damson pulp. Boil it, stirring it well till it is thick. Keep the fire low, and boil the pulp very slowly. After the cheese has thickened well, leave off stirring; but it must boil quite to a candy, and may take seven hours. Put in the kernels a few minutes before the damson cheese is taken off the fire. The cheese will be done when it leaves the sides of the pan. A peck and a half of damsons will make ten pints of cheese. Cover the moulds when cold with paper dipped in brandy.

Brandy Cherries.—To every pound of Morello cherries, stalked but not stoned, add three-quarters of a pound of best loaf sugar. Take a few cherries, bruise them, and take as much juice from them as will make the sugar into a very thick syrup. Fill wide-mouthed bottles with the cherries, and prick each cherry all over with a fine needle. Let the syrup get quite cold, then pour it on the cherries, and fill up the bottles with good brandy.

Brandy Peaches—Peel the peaches carefully with a silver dessert-knife, and as you do so put each peach into cold water. Choose a deep stone jar, put into it one pound of peaches covered with three-quarters of a pound of sifted sugar. Fill up the jar with good brandy. Set the jar in a pan of cold water on the fire, and let it gradually heat till the brandy is nearly boiling. Then let it get cold and tie up the jar closely.

A STORE-ROOM for apples and pears should be cool, though frost-proof, slightly moist, and well ventilated, though free from draughts. Adjacent apples should not be in contact with each other. If very choice, it is wise to wrap each apple in tissue paper. The fruit should be hand-picked, and placed in the store-room when quite dry, and any specimens that show signs of rottenness should be removed directly they are recognized.

Messrs. Bunyard, of Maidstone, have built some fruit-houses which admirably fulfil the desired conditions. The following instructions for erecting a similar storehouse are given by Mr. George Bunyard.

First level the soil and dig out holes for the corners large enough to admit brick piers 14 inches by 14 inches, or stones about 1 foot square; fix an iron dowel in the centre to receive the corner posts of the structure. Some provision for air (air-bricks), or an aperture covered outside and inside with perforated zinc, should be provided just above the ground line, and if over 20 feet long an extra foundation should be put in at the half distance to hold another support.

Make the main posts 6 feet long, 6 inches square, and prepare a hole in the foot to receive the dowel mentioned above. This will keep the framework firm. The main ground plate should be $4\frac{1}{2}$ inches by 3 inches, and the top plate of the same size. Support and steady in the usual way with quartering $4\frac{1}{2}$ inches by 3 inches, and when this is fixed, choose a dry day, and pitch, tar, or cold creosote the lower plates and all the woodwork 2 feet from the ground to protect from damp : this quartering should show an even outside face to secure the matchboard.

The cheapest material for the outside covering will be $\frac{3}{4}$-inch matchboard, and it may as well be fixed outside the rafters as well. Pitchboard $4\frac{1}{2}$ inches by 1 inch, rafters 3 inches by 2 inches.

Inside Bonds from one side to the other, $4\frac{1}{2}$ inches by 3 inches. If stout they are useful to hold planks, on which baskets can be placed overhead in the roof, space. In order to receive the side thatch, a board is attached round the door-plates and at the corners, 6 inches wide, from the ground to eaves, in which the thatch is placed upright, and it is kept in position by lateral splines of wood 3 inches by 1 inch.

The Roof Thatch may be 18 inches thick on the roof and 6 inches at the sides, and where it can be procured, carex or reed is strongest and most lasting, but it may be of wheat straw or heather. The thatch at the sides should be 6 inches thick.

Both an inside and outside door should be provided, and they must be made to fit closely to exclude draughts.

A FRUIT-ROOM.

fruit shall not touch the wooden shelves. In the centre of the fruit-house a narrow table with a raised edge made of lengths of matchboard, set on trestles, is useful to set up exhibition collections or to show special samples. Baskets of fruit can be set under this for early use.

Floor.—The best possible floor is the natural earth—paved surfaces are apt to become too dry. The latest sorts should be stored on the lowest shelf.

Names.—Provide slips of zinc 4 inches long, turn up one end 1 inch, at an angle of 45°, and then slit this angle three times, and bend it so that it will hold a neat card; the other end can be slipped under the straw.

From their fruit-house, constructed on these lines, Messrs. Bunyard have put up 80 dishes of fresh clean apples at the Temple Shows at the end of May.

Pears.—If pears constitute the bulk of the store, the fruit-house should be rather drier and rather warmer than in the case of apples. In either case, the winter temperature should not fall below 40° F., and the summer temperature should not rise above 60° F.

A very convenient method of storing apples and pears is in flat trays, such as those known as Orr's, of which Mr. White, of Bedford, holds the patent rights. The fruit is placed direct in these as picked from the tree, and the trays are carried to the fruit-house as fast as they are filled.

Medlars should be picked in November, preferably after the frost has touched them. Their stalks should be dipped in strong lime, and the fruits buried in boxes of wet bran, no two medlars touching, and placed in the fruit-house.

Walnuts should be removed from their outer rinds, and at once placed in an earthen jar. Cover them with three inches of sawdust, and place them in a cool cellar or fruit-house.

Filberts, Cobs and Hedge Nuts, for storing, should be gathered just before they slip their husks—though they must be so ripe as to do so at the slightest force. They should be dried before storing, or the husks will become mouldy. They may then be treated as advised for walnuts, or they may be placed in a jar and sprinkled over with salt.

Gathering and Drying Herbs.—Herbs should usually be picked just before they flower, and, their roots having been cut off, they should be tied into bundles and quickly sun-dried. These bundles may then be tied in paper bags and hung in a dry room, or they may be powdered and bottled. Lavender should be cut as soon as the flowers are fully open. It should then be dried in the shade, and stored in a dry room.

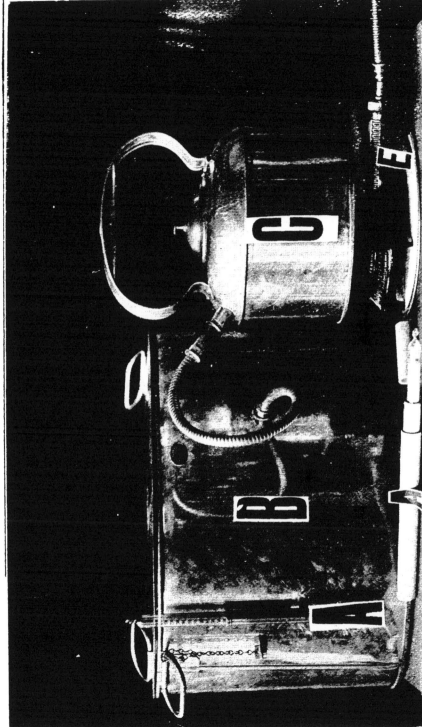

THE BOTTLING OF FRUIT AND VEGETABLES

THE value of fruits bottled whole in such a way that they retain their natural form as well as their natural flavour is becoming more and more recognized, and fortunately science has kept space with the spread of this recognition, so that it is a perfectly simple matter for the owner of the smallest garden to bottle his fruit at the most trifling cost and trouble. The methods adopted have for their object the destruction of the germs present in the fruit, through whose activity fermentation and decomposition usually result, and the subsequent exclusion of germs from the vessels in which the fruit is being preserved. Glass bottles with air-tight stoppers are usually employed for this purpose, and several excellent varieties are in the market. In practically all of them, the top fits on the wide open mouth of the bottle and presses on a rubber ring. The tops are usually either held down by a metal screw ring or by a spring clip or wire bail. Of the bottles here illustrated, the Climax, May Queen, and Empress are manufactured by the Rylands Glass Company, of Barnsby; whilst the others are dealt in by Messrs. E. Lee and Company, of Maidstone. Messrs. Lee are also responsible for an admirable apparatus or boiling pan for sterilizing the fruit or other product. This apparatus serves not only for the purposes of fruit bottling, but is also serviceable for sterilizing milk and for certain other culinary purposes. Select ripe fruit, removing any that are unsound, and, having washed the bottles,

RYLAND'S FRUIT BOTTLES.

Empress.   Climax.   May Queen.

place the fruit therein—packing the bottles full to the shoulder. Pour in cold water or cold syrup (from a table-spoonful to half a pound of sugar to the pint of water) so as to fill the bottles to the brim. Place the indiarubber ring round the ledge on the neck of the bottle, place the disc upon it, and loosely arrange

LEE S FRUIT BOTTLING BOILER AND FRUIT BOTTLES

the screw-top, if that method be adopted, as free outlet must be left for steam to escape. Take a pan, such as Lee's sterilizing apparatus includes, and place cold water in it of such a depth as shall reach the shoulders of the bottles which are now to be placed in the pan. Heat until the water in the pan has a temperature of between 155° and 160° F., and this temperature is to be maintained until the bottles are removed. The bottles are to be lifted out singly and the covers at once screwed down, or locked by the spring or lever, according to the make of bottle. They should be cooled as quickly as possible. Apples and pears should be peeled, cut, and cored, and placed in cold water directly they are cored. All stone fruit should be stoned before bottling. The time for which the bottles should remain in the pan, at a temperature of 155° to 160° F., varies. Cherries, rhubarb, small plums, gooseberries and currants require about twenty minutes; tomatoes, half an hour; apricots, three-quarters of an hour; and pears, an hour.

Mushrooms and carrots may be bottled in the same way as fruit, but the bottles containing them should be left in the pan of heated water for an hour and a half. Green peas, asparagus and French beans, if first placed in boiling water for five minutes, may be bottled in like way, the bottles remaining in the pan for an hour.

To make Fruit Syrups.—Mash the fruit (raspberries, currants, strawberries, blackberries, etc.), and allow it to remain, loosely covered, in a warm place for three days. Then pass the juice through a muslin strainer, and add a pound of sugar to every half-pound of juice. Boil until the sugar is dissolved. Cool and bottle, corking securely.

THE DRYING OF FRUIT AND VEGETABLES

BY means of an evaporator, or drier, a number of fruit and vegetables may be preserved by the removal of the moisture which they contain. Quite cheap evaporators are now to be obtained, such as the *Quorn*, of Messrs. Lumley, of the Minories, London. As the makers of the various evaporating appliances supply full instructions for their use, it is not necessary here to give more than the briefest summary of the treatment to be adopted in drying one or two typical fruits and vegetables.

The method of preparing apples to be evaporated is as follows : —

After the apples have been pared, cored, and sliced, they are placed in a tub of perfectly clean water, containing a small quantity of salt, which prevents oxidation and discoloration. They are then cut once vertically, and all bruises, specks, and parings trimmed away to produce the well-known apple-rings of commerce. These are placed thinly on one of the trays of the evaporator and entered at the lower end of the upper flue. Sometimes a little sulphur may be sprinkled on the furnace with great advantage for the purpose of bleaching the rings. The first tray remains in the position just mentioned until the second tray is ready to be placed under the first tray which will be in four or five minutes; the third tray is then filled in the usual manner, and placed under the second tray, and when the fourth tray is ready the first three trays are pushed forward in the flue, and the fourth tray takes the place of No. 1, and so on until the top flue is full. On the arrival of the first tray at the upper end of the flue, the contents are examined, and those that are sufficiently dried are removed, and the remainder turned over and returned down the lower and cooler flue. In many cases, one tray will hold the whole of the contents (which are nearly dried) of two or three trays, the empty ones being taken away to be again filled with fresh fruit. The degree of heat used for drying apples is from 175° to 240° F.; and the time occupied varies from two to four hours, according to the variety of the apple, but from two to two and a half hours is the usual time. Whole apples require a much longer time, eight to ten hours, according to size and variety.

Plums are dried in the same manner, except that they are placed in the evaporator at once. They should be graded according to size, and be uniformly ripe. During the process of evaporation plums ought to be removed from the evaporator once or twice for the purpose of cooling them and toughening the skin, and so prevent bursting, which they are liable to do, because the skin does not allow the moisture in the fruit to freely escape when first placed in the machine. As soon as the plums commence to shrivel all danger of bursting is past, and they may then remain in the evaporator until dry. The time required for plums is from six to ten hours, and the temperature requisite 240° to 300° F. Plums may be steamed for a few minutes and then split in half, thus entirely dispensing with the cooling process, and considerably reducing the length of time required in drying. 100 pounds of fresh plums will give about 30 pounds of dried.

Apricots are simply cut in two, the stones being taken out, and the fruit then dried just like apples, at from 240° to 250° F. They take from two to three hours to dry. From 100 pounds of the fresh fruit, 10 to 12 pounds of dried will result.

Pears for drying purposes ought not to be quite ripe. They are peeled, and either dried whole, or, more generally, are divided, and the seed-vessels cut out, the stems being left on. They then require steaming for eight or ten minutes, and are filled in from the bottom upwards. The temperature used is 212° to 240° F., and the pears will take five to seven hours to dry if divided, or seven to nine hours if whole. From 100 pounds of fresh pears 12 to 16 pounds of dried ones will be obtained. When preparing the pears before drying, the flavour will be improved if a little sugar be added to the water in which they are cooked, and to this may be put the juice of the removed seed-vessels and peelings.

Vegetables require, in addition to the peeling, slicing, or cutting up, to be steamed or cooked for five to seven minutes before they are dried. This is necessary in order to keep their colour and to prevent their becoming hard. When dried on a small scale the cooking in boiling water is generally sufficient. Like apples, vegetables are always filled in from below upwards.

French beans are cut into strips by a special machine, and cooked for a few minutes. A little soda added to the water helps to preserve their bright green colour. The time required for drying is from three-quarters to one hour. Temperature 150° to 160° F. 100 pounds of fresh beans giving 10 to 12 pounds of dry.

Peas require simply shelling and a few minutes' cooking. They should not be quite ripe, and are laid thinly on the trays. They take from one to one and a half hours to dry. Temperature 212° to 220° F. 100 pounds of green pods will yield about 10 to 12 pounds of dried peas.

" Blessing of your heart, you brew good ale."

" It illuminateth the face, warmeth the blood, and maketh it course from the inwards to the parts extreme."

" A quart of ale is a dish for a king."

" Sir, I have now in my cellar ten tun of the best ale in Staffordshire ; 'tis smooth as oil, sweet as milk, clear as amber, and strong as brandy ; and will be just fourteen years old the fifth day of next March, old style."

ONE of the finest pamphlets ever issued in this country is William Cobbett's "Cottage Economy." Even now it affords good stimulating reading, and might still serve as a wise protest against the pietistic and other cant of the times. The object of the little book was first to emphasize the sound doctrines that no nation ever was or ever will be permanently great if it consists to any large extent of wretched and miserable families; that a family to be happy must usually be well supplied with food and raiment ; and that it is to blaspheme God to suppose that He created men to be miserable, to hunger, to thirst, and to perish with cold in the midst of that abundance which is the fruit of their own labour. The second object of the book was to convey to the families of the labouring classes in particular such information as to the preparation of food, the selection

of clothes and furniture, and the general management of homes as his wisdom and sound judgment
dictated. All through the book runs a steady stream
of common sense far removed from the slushy cant
so prevalent in works of the kind. "A couple of
flitches of bacon are worth fifty thousand Methodist
sermons and religious tracts. They are great
softeners of the temper and promoters of domestic
harmony." "Oak tables, bedsteads, and stools,
chairs of oak or of yew-tree, and never a bit of
miserable deal board. Things of this sort ought to
last several lifetimes. A labourer ought to inherit
from his great-grandfather something besides his
toil." "Nowadays the labourers, and especially the
female part of them, have fallen into the taste of
niceness in food and finery in dress; a quarter of a
bellyful and rags are the consequence. The food
of their choice is high-priced, and the dress of their
choice is showy and flimsy, so that to-day they are
ladies, and to-morrow ragged as sheep with the
scab." A healthy attitude towards the plain and
the wholesome and the genuine marks the whole
book. Among other things ardently desired by
Cobbett was the extension of the practice of the
home brewing of honest beer, and he denounced
the growing habit of tea-drinking with a vigour
that time and results have shown was not misplaced.
He looked upon tea-drinking as a destroyer of
health, an enfeebler of the frame, an engenderer
of effeminacy and laziness, a debaucher of youth,

and a maker of misery for old age. And he could scarce find adequate vent for his impatience of what he rightly considered the everlasting dawdling about with the slops of the tea-tackle, or for his pity for the labourer who, instead of cheerfully and vigorously doing a morning's work on the strength of a breakfast of bread, bacon, and beer, has to force his tea-sodden limbs along under the sweat of feebleness, and at night to return to the wretched tea-kettle once more. How different, says Cobbett, is the fate of that man who has made his wife brew beer instead of making tea !

It has been said and often quoted that there is good beer, and better beer, but no bad beer. The present writer's experience is that there is beer so bad that few drinks can rival it for disagreeableness in taste and effects ; stuff which should never be called by the same name as that transparent, brown or amber, vinous fluid, " bright as a sunbeam," free from acidity, flatness and insipidity, which alone is worthy the name of beer.

To make good beer requires good materials, care, cleanliness, and method. Given those, failure should be impossible. The water should be good, soft water being usually to be preferred ; the malt fresh and full of flour ; the hops bright, yellowish-green in colour, with a pleasant brisk fragrance, and free from leaves and bits of stem ; and the various tubs, boilers, and other appliances scrupulously clean. The several temperatures should be taken with a proper thermometer, and not guessed, as that way many disasters lie.

Spring and autumn are the seasons most suited for brewing, as at other times it is difficult to keep the temperature within the proper limits. Four bushels of ground or bruised malt are placed in a wooden " mash tun," and twenty-two gallons of

BARNETT AND FOSTER'S SPILE-DRAWER.

water at a temperature of 170° F. are added thereto. This is well stirred for half an hour, and then another eighteen gallons of water at 170° F. are added, and the stirring is continued for half an hour longer. Cover the mash tun for a couple of hours, and then draw off the infusion or wort through a hole in the bottom, protected by a strainer, so that the malt itself remains behind in the mash tun. Next add to the malt thirty gallons of water at 185° F. Stir for half an hour, let it stand for an hour, and then draw off as before. Next add eighteen gallons of water at 200° F. to the malt, stir for ten minutes, and draw off half an hour later. The three washings may be all mixed together if a good ale of average strength is desired, or the third washing may be separately treated so as to make a light table ale, or they may be all three separately treated so as to form three ales varying from very strong to very light, the former having considerable keeping quality. In any case, it is imperative that the minimum of time be lost in transferring the wort to the copper. It should be boiled for an hour and a half, and the hops (varying from one pound in the case of a mild table ale to six or seven pounds in the case of very bitter ales, three pounds being a good average amount) added, the boiling being continued for half an hour longer. The wort is then passed through a strainer into large, shallow tubs to cool, the depth of liquid not exceeding four inches. It is next poured into fermenting tuns (casks with one head removed do nicely), which must not be more than half-filled. The yeast (at the rate of a pint to the barrel of thirty-six gallons of wort) is to be mixed with a little of the wort which has been heated to 85° F. As soon as this portion shows signs of general per-meation by the process of fermentation it is to be added to the main body of wort, which is to be at a temperature of 60° F. Stir it well, and then allow it to stand. As soon as a yeasty appearance is noticed in the head which rises to the surface, skim it off every two days until no more yeast appears—usually a week or more from the start. Then draw off the clear ale into casks, filling them completely, bung them securely, and place them in a cool cellar. It may then be kept for from one to twelve months, or longer, according to its quality and strength. Ale or beer should be tapped a week before it is required to draw any from the cask in order that it may have time to settle.

Finally, the ale-wife may be referred to the appeal of Dr. King—

> " *O Girzy, Girzy ! when thou go'st to brew,*
> *Consider well what you're about to do ;*
> *Be very wise, very sedately think,*
> *That what you're going now to make is drink.*
> *Consider who must drink that drink, and then*
> *What 'tis to have the praise of honest men."*

CIDER

THE processes of cider-making are discussed and explained by the present writer in Thomas's " Book of the Apple," one of the volumes in the series of " Handbooks of Practical Gardening." The following short summary must here suffice. The apples, properly selected and properly ripened by being thinly piled on boards or straw in an airy, sunny place, should be torn and crushed in a cider mill, and the juice pressed out by means of a screw-press. This crude juice should then be carefully strained through a fine-meshed filter, in order to remove any cellular tissue or other matter in suspension. The expressed apple juice, having been freed by filtration from undissolved solids, is next to be subjected to the process of fermentation, that is, the conversion of its sugar into alcohol. For this purpose, it should be exposed to the air in large open vats, or in casks with the bung-hole left open. All the apple juice that is to be fermented in one vat or cask should be placed in it within twelve hours from the time of placing any therein. The specific gravity should be taken daily by means of a brewer's hydrometer, about six-sevenths of the total solids consisting of sugar. Approximately, the sugar gives about half its weight of alcohol, and it has been found that each decrease of one-hundredth in the specific gravity of the fluid during fermentation corresponds to the conversion of two per cent. of sugar into one per cent. of alcohol. The scum which rises to the surface of the liquid must be skimmed off two or three times daily, and, as soon as this frothy crust ceases to rise, the cider still in process of active fermentation is to be drawn off with great care by means of a rubber syphon or pump and hose into perfectly clean casks. It is well to rinse out the casks with water of about the same temperature as that of the cider which is to fill them, as a sudden drop of heat is very injurious. The casks of cider should be kept at a steady temperature of about 50° F.

If the open vat system of "purging" is unavailable, then the cider is to be placed in casks with the bung-holes left open, the cask being kept full to the brim by frequent additions of clear old cider. The scum in this case overflows at the bung-holes until the purging process is complete. Subsequently the cork is to be inserted, a bent glass tube being passed through its centre, ending outwardly in a basin of water. The excess of carbonic acid gas is thus enabled to escape. As soon as the conversion of sugar into alcohol is almost complete, the cider should be carefully filtered at a low temperature by means of a Filtre Rapide or other suitable strainer (which must not consist of charcoal, sand, or clay), and stored in clean air-tight casks in a cool place, being previously pasteurized if the process be thought desirable or worth while. The cider must then be left for a time in order to ripen, that is, to develop bouquet and vinosity. If intended for bottling, that process may be performed in the following spring, or preferably in the following autumn. All antiseptics, preservatives, and artificial flavouring agents should be avoided as suggestions of the devil. Scrupulous cleanliness of fruit, filters, presses, mills, vats and casks should make the two first-named possible additions unnecessary, and careful selection of fruit should make the idea of artificial flavouring an obvious absurdity.

" It should be clear like the tears of a penitent, so that a man may see distinctly to the bottom of the glass; its colour should represent the greenness of a buffalo's horn; when drunk it should descend impetuously like thunder; sweet-tasted as an almond; creeping like a squirrel; leaping like a roebuck; strong like the building of a Cistercian monastery; glittering like a spark of fire; subtle like the logic of the schools of Paris; and delicate as fine silk.

" Often the blind piper would pay us a visit and taste our gooseberry wine, for the making of which we had lost neither the receipt nor the reputation."

*G*ENERAL *Principles.*—In making wines from fresh British fruit, the fruit should be quite mature, yet as fresh in reality as in name; and too much care cannot be taken in removing all stems, leaves, unripe or diseased fruits, and other refuse which would certainly affect the taste, appearance, and keeping power of the ultimate wine. As soon as possible after being gathered, the fruit is to be placed in a tub or other vessel, and submitted to the process of crushing or bruising. It is then thrown into a wooden vat, the water added, and the mixture allowed to stand for from one to three days, according to the variety of wine and other circumstances. During this period of maceration, the mixture is to be frequently stirred by means of a wooden stirrer. The liquid portion is then drawn or strained off, the residuary pulp being placed in hair bags and subjected to pressure. In the case of raisins and other dried fruits, it is customary to chop them into small pieces, and to soak them in water for twelve hours before crushing them. The liquid which is thus squeezed out is added to the rest of the liquid and placed in another vat of wood or earthenware, the sugar and cream of tartar being added, and the whole well stirred for twenty minutes. Yeast should then be added, when any is required, and a temperature of about 60° F. maintained. For about three days—or until most of the sugar is converted into alcohol, as shown by the saccharometer—the mixture is to be kept closely covered by means of mats or other coverings. It is, during this time, to be frequently stirred and its surface skimmed.

It is then carefully to be run off into casks, the latter to be filled to the brim, and the wine allowed to work over or "purge" at the partly open bung-holes. The casks are to be kept con_ stantly filled up with juice, and in about a fort_ night the rectified spirit is to be added, if such addition is thought desirable. The casks are then to be bunged securely and left for a month, when they are to be again filled up and re-bunged. Six weeks later they should be pegged or spiled, and a little wine drawn off to ascertain if it be clear. If it is quite clear, it may be racked off—preferably by means of a syphon—into other casks or into bottles for storage. If, however, it is not yet clear, the casks must be bunged up and left for another fortnight, or the wine may be fined by the addition of isinglass—half an ounce to the hogshead—previously dissolved in a little cold water and diluted with a pint of wine. This fining solution is to be thoroughly mixed with the wine in the casks by means of a

A GROUP OF DRINKING-GLASSES.

clean broom-handle. In a short time the isinglass, with the objectionable particles in the wine, sinks to the bottom, and so enables the clear liquid to be drawn off. It should then be stored for at least six months in a cellar having a temperature of about 56° F.

Racking is best performed by means of a syphon,

though the wine may be—and commonly is—
drawn off by a tap. In the latter case the tap
should be inserted two or three days before the
wine is to be drawn off, thus affording it time to
re-settle. If it is not convenient to rack off the
wine into a second cask, it may be drawn into a

A GROUP OF ANCIENT BOTTLES.

clean tub or vat, and returned to the same cask
after it has been thoroughly cleaned, and turned
bung-hole downwards over an ounce of sulphur,
which is to be burnt so as to fill the cask with the
fumes, the wine being at once returned and the
bung secured.

It is of the utmost consequence in wine-making

that every implement, cask, tub, tap, bottle, and cork, be scrupulously clean before they come into contact with the wine ; and in bottling it is essential that the bottles be perfectly dry.

A SIMPLE FRUIT-MILL.

Among the most important and useful appliances for the home wine-maker are the following : barrels, vats, bottles, corks, taps, pegs, mallet, cork-squeezer, fruit-crusher, wine-press, straining bags,

CORK-DRIVER.

and syphon. These may be obtained of Messrs. Lumley, of 1, America Square, Minories, London ; or Messrs. Barnett and Foster, of Eagle Wharf Road, London.

I cannot too strongly urge the reader to be loyal

to her country and to good taste in her wine-making; and to confine herself chiefly to the making of simple British wines from British fruit with British names. Nothing is more objectionable than to brand wines as British ports, British sherries, English claret, and so on. It is almost as insufferable as the labelling of writers as Belgian Shakespeares, English Molières, French Fieldings, and the rest.

I will describe the method of preparing a few typical wines, and then indicate the several classes in which the various British wines may be arranged.

To make Gooseberry Wine.—Take six pounds of perfectly ripe gooseberries, and treat them as directed in the section on general principles. Allow one gallon of soft, filtered, or distilled water ; four pounds of sugar, previously made into a syrup with part of the water ; and one and a quarter ounces of cream of tartar. One or two ounces of rectified spirits of wine may be added. Each of these several ingredients is to be added at that stage of the fermentation indicated in the section on general principles.

To make Sparkling Gooseberry Wine.—Proceed as in the last recipe ; but do not allow the fermentation quite to complete itself before bottling the wine. Add to each bottle a tiny piece of sugar of about the size of a pea. Use good strong bottles, and secure the corks by wiring them. It is sometimes desirable to hasten fermentation in the vat by placing therein a small piece of toast spread on both sides with ale yeast.

To make Lemon Wine.—Take five pounds of peeled lemons and the sliced peel of four lemons,

A GROUP OF MODERN BOTTLES.

and proceed as in making gooseberry wine, but allow only three and a half pounds of sugar and add no cream of tartar. The pips should be removed before the fruit is crushed.

To make Cowslip Wine.—Prepare a simple wine

after the manner of making gooseberry wine, employing one pound of raisins, four pounds of sugar, and one ounce of cream of tartar to the gallon of water. When active fermentation has nearly ceased, a few weeks before racking, add two quarts of bruised cowslip flowers. Then complete the making of the wine in the usual way.

To make Rhubarb Wine.—Take five pounds of rhubarb stalks, cut them into small pieces, and proceed as in making either gooseberry or sparkling gooseberry wine, but no cream of tartar should be added, and only three pounds of sugar should be allowed to the gallon.

To make Date Wine.—Take six pounds of stoned dates, and proceed as in making gooseberry wine, but no sugar is to be added.

The Merissah of the Berbers is a wine made from dates to which a small quantity of maize has been added.

To make Damson Wine.—Take five pounds of ripe stoned damsons; crush them and one-tenth of their stones, and boil them in a gallon of water. Then proceed as in making gooseberry wine, but only allow three pounds of sugar.

Mead, or Metheglin—for the distinction between them is difficult to determine—was the chief alcoholic beverage of the earliest inhabitants of Britain, and the maker of the mead was the eleventh person in order of precedence at the ancient courts of the Welsh princes. Mead is usually supposed to have been the fermented wine obtained from the liquor formed by boiling honeycombs with water, whereas metheglin was prepared from honey and water, with or without the addition of hops or spices.

To make Spiced Metheglin.—Boil for an hour a mixture of one gallon of water and three pounds of

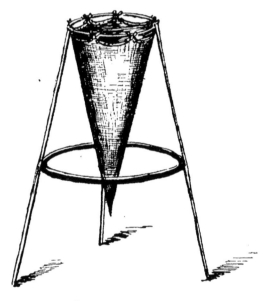

A WINE FILTER-BAG.

honey, taking off the scum as it forms. Allow the mixture to stand for twenty-hour hours, add yeast on toast, and proceed as directed in the section on the general principles of wine-making. When the active fermentation is subsiding, a few weeks before racking the mead, hang into the liquid within the barrel an open woven bag of mixed spices, an ounce each of crushed ginger, cloves, allspice, and coriander seeds.

To make Metheglin with Hops.—Boil half an ounce of hops in water, and allow it cool. Pour three quarts of warm water on three pounds of honey, stir, and allow the mixture to stand for twelve hours. Then add the hops and the water in which they were boiled, together with a piece of toast spread on both sides with yeast. Allow the mixture to ferment, and proceed as directed in the section on the general principles of wine-making. Add no ingredients beyond those named above.

Hydromel is but another name for metheglin, the word implying a product of the fermentation of a mixture of honey and water.

To make American Mead.—Take a barrel of cider, fresh from the apple-press, and place therein twenty or thirty pounds of drained honeycombs. The next day add sufficient honey to raise the specific gravity to such a point that an egg will float in the mixture. It is then to be treated in the manner suggested in the paragraph on the general principles of wine-making, the only further addition being half a gallon of rectified spirits.

To make Ginger Beer.—Take five gallons of boiling water and pour it on five pounds of lump sugar, five lemons sliced and without their pips, five ounces of bruised ginger, and five ounces of cream of tartar. Strain off when the liquid is cool enough, and add five table-spoonfuls of brewer's yeast. Let the ginger beer stand all night, and then strain again as carefully as possible. Add the white of one egg before bottling the ginger beer, and put the beer in well-washed champagne bottles. It will be ready in one week. Brewer's yeast should, if possible, be used, but if none can be had, two ounces of German yeast may be substituted for it.—*J. R.*

To make Spruce Beer.—Mince a quantity of young sprouts of the spruce, and boil them with twenty times their volume of water and an ounce of sugar to the pint of shoots. Allow to cool and proceed as in making ginger beer.

"*He wanted to make a memorandum in his pocket-book; it was about spruce beer. Mr. Knightley had been telling him something about brewing spruce beer, and he wanted to put it down.*"

Certain other Wines.—Currant (red, white, or black), cherry, raspberry, mulberry, whortleberry, blackberry, apple, grape, and elderberry wines are made after the manner of gooseberry wine.

Sloe wine and green gooseberry wine, which latter is not recommended, are made like damson wine.

Raisin and fig wines are made as date wine is made.

Orange wine is made as lemon wine. Apricot, clary, elderflower, ginger, juniper, and gilliflower wines are made after the manner prescribed for cowslip wine.

It is often thought desirable to add to wines the flavour of spices or herbs other than those essentially used in the making of the wine. In such a case, the spices should be placed in a muslin bag and suspended in the wine when active fermentation is subsiding, as suggested in the directions for making. Commonly for elderberry wine, a mixture of crushed ginger, cinnamon, cloves, and mace—of each half an ounce to the gallon—is employed, and for whortle-berry wine a mixture of lavender, rosemary, and ginger.

British wines have earned their bad name partly through the careless manner in which they are usually prepared, unclean bottles, corks, casks, and vats being commonly used ; and partly through the absurdly short space of time allowed to elapse between making and drinking. No wine is fit to drink under two years from the time of its manu-facture, and most wines should be kept in bottle much longer than is customary.

THE DISTILLING OF WATERS AND CORDIALS

THERE is no occupation that comes nearer to the work of gods than this occupation of distilling. By the application of fire, the purest of the elements, we separate from gross, substantial bodies those subtle essences which alone gave them distinction and charm. The distiller can but smile at the impotence of those who are unable to conceive the possibility of a post-physical human existence, for, day by day, as he stands before his stills, he sees the miracle performed whereby the spiritual, the essential, is separated and continues to exist apart from the material body in which it previously dwelt.

The work is worthy of fine natures, and should be undertaken with a mind full of reverence.

The practice of distillation dates back to very early times, the oil of cedar mentioned by Dioscorides having been obtained by boiling the oleoresin with water, and condensing the vapour of the oil in sheep's wool spread on sticks placed across the top of the vessel. But more elaborate stills, consisting of cucurbit, alembic (or head) and receiver, were in use in times not much more recent. Water-baths, sand-baths, and other means for regulating the heat applied to the body of the still were used as early as

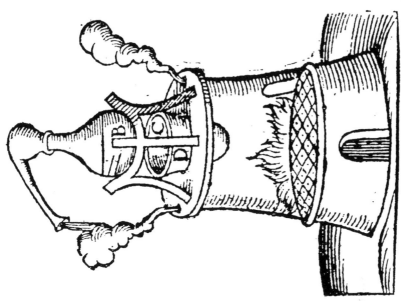

DISTILLING BY HEAT OF STEAM.

(*From Peter Morwyng's "Treasure of Enonymus," 1559.*)

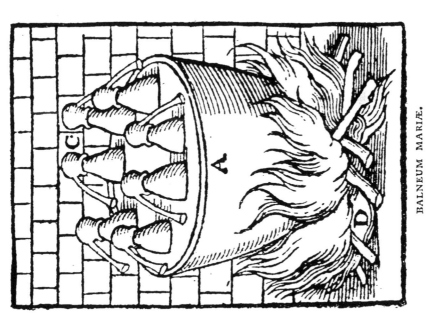

BALNEUM MARIÆ.

(*From Peter Morwyng's "Treasure of Enonymus," 1559.*)

the eighth century by the Arabians. It was at about this time, also, that distillation of alcohol was first practised.

The distillation of pure alcohol from mixtures containing it, is really only worth attempting under somewhat elaborate conditions, and on a fairly large scale. The distillation of essences and aromatic waters, and of a number of liqueurs may, however, be quite well practised on the domestic scale. A perfectly made tin-lined copper still, with pewter or copper head, neck, and worm, the latter fitting in a wood or metal tub, is the principle article required. It is desirable to have the cucurbit fitted with a perforated water-bath, or metallic basket, to contain the herbs or seeds which are to be heated in the water or alcohol. These substances, thus saved from contact with the inner surface of the cucurbit, are not liable to burn or to stick. For certain things, also, it is desirable to be provided with an unperforated bain-marie when it is wished not to subject the materials to a heat quite equal to the temperature of boiling water.

All the joints of the still and the tubes connected with it must be absolutely vapour-proof, or the subtle gases of the spirits and essences will discover the outlet and escape. The water in the tub containing the worm must be kept cold, a few jugfuls being drawn from its surface at intervals and replaced by fresh cold water. Where possible, fresh plants should be used for distilling purposes, as they more

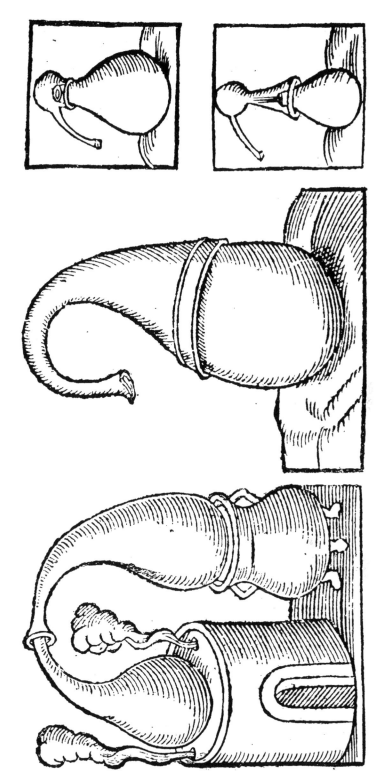

SOME OLD DISTILLING VESSELS.

readily yield their essential oils than is usually the case with dried plants.

Aromatic Waters.—For the distilling of simple aromatic waters about a gallon of water should be allowed to four pounds of the fresh herb, or one pound of the dry herb, and about two quarts should be distilled over. Peppermint water, damask-rose water, orange-flower water, spearmint water, and elder-flower water are prepared in this way. For dill water, caraway water, fennel water, and cinnamon water, a pound of the bruised fruit is mixed with two gallons of water, and one gallon is distilled over.

Rosemary Water is made by mixing a gallon of water, eleven and a half gallons of rectified spirit, and fourteen pounds of rosemary flowers and leaves, and slowly distilling off ten gallons over the water-bath.

Simple Lavender Water is made in the same way, substituting lavender flowers for the rosemary flowers and leaves.

Beauty Water is made by mixing half a gallon of rectified spirits, a gallon of water, a pound of the flowering tops of thyme and a pound of those of marjoram, and distilling off a gallon.

The Distilling of Essences.—The following is a summary of the directions given by M. Deroy of Paris, a well-known manufacturer of excellent stills and other appliances connected with distilling, for the distilling of essences or essential oils.

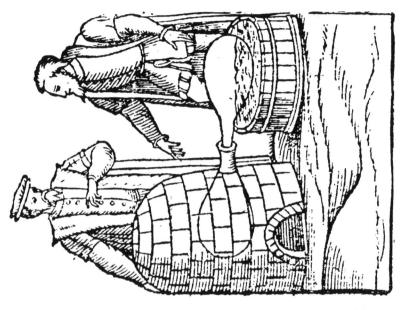

ALCHEMIST WITH HIS SERVANT.

(*From Peter Morwyng's "Treasure of Enonymus," 1559.*)

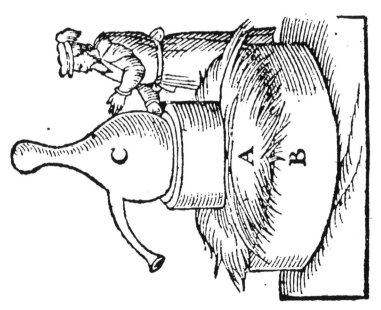

DISTILLING BY HEAT OF FERMENTING MANURE.

(*From Peter Morwyng's "Treasure of Enonymus," 1559.*)

The generality of plants give their maximum of essence when they are dealt with in their fresh condition. Some few, however, produce more when they are dry. The produce of the same kind may vary for divers reasons. The moment of its harvest and the atmospheric conditions under which it is effected, the nature of the soil, the quality of the plants, and their more or less favourable exposal, exercise a sensible influence upon the production.

Substances, previously either cut to pieces, incised, rasped, ground, or crushed according to their nature, are placed in water of ordinary temperature for macerating.

The proportion of water used is mostly of three to four times the weight of the substance. The length of time for soaking varies from twelve to forty-eight hours according to the dryness and the divided state of the substance. Some light essences extracted from fresh flowers (from roses, for example) are obtained without previous maceration.

The matter is placed in the still with the water into which it has been macerated. Sea-salt is sometimes added for the purpose of retarding the point of boiling. It is known that salted water only boils at 108° Centigrade, say about 229° Fahrenheit.

Those who follow this method, which is the one most generally employed when it is a question of exhausting plants which contain rather heavy oils, certify that the essences separate themselves more

"This instrument, named the Pellicane, which is a Vessell for Circulating, serveth to none other ende and purpose, than for to Circulate the Quintessence, which by the Arte of dystilling is drawen."

A 16TH-CENTURY STILL, WITH CONDENSER JACKET TO HELM OF STILL.

easily if distilling is effected at a little over 100° C. (water boiling-point).

Those who criticize this proceeding pretend that it has the disadvantage of injuring the quality of the essences obtained.

Thus the necessary quantity of sea salt required for the complete salting of the water is rarely used, which is to say about 40 per cent. ; the majority of distillers limit themselves, according to the case in hand, to putting in 20 per cent. and sometimes only from 12 to 15 per cent., considering this a sufficient quantity to obtain a satisfactory result.

During the course of the distillation, the water in the refrigerator should be renewed by ordinary means when distilling essences which remain fluid at a normal temperature. Whilst, as for the crystallizable essences such as aniseed, China-aniseed, caraway, fennel, peppermint, and roses, care should be taken to keep the worm at about 30° or 40° Centigrade.

Distilling can be effected by steam or direct fire heat, by taking the precaution in the latter case to place an interior grating in the copper so as to hinder the substances from sticking to the bottom.

The aqueous vapours mixed with those of the essences become condensed in the worm, and the produce of these condensations is gathered in a special vase, known as a Florentine receiver, where the oil becomes separated from the distilled water,

STILLS AT THE WORKS OF THE LONDON ESSENCE CO

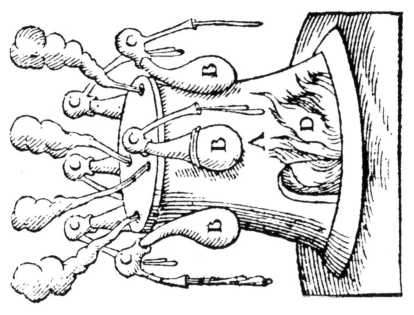

FURNACE WITH STILLS.

(*From Peter Morwyng's "Treasure of Enonymus," 1559.*)

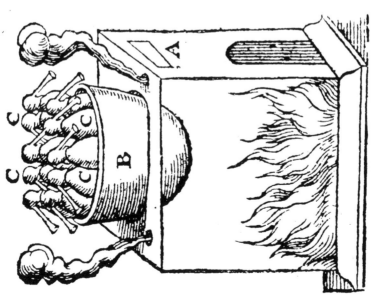

BALNEUM MARIÆ.

(*From Peter Morwyng's "Treasure of Enonymus," 1559.*)

by reason of the different densities of the two bodies. According to the nature of the essence, whether lighter or heavier than water, this recipient is supplied either in its upper or lower part with a side spout, by which the overflow of the water passes and leaves the essence to accumulate in the vase in measure as it is produced.

Distilling is continued until the water runs out at the outlet of the worm in a limpid state. By this sign it is known that the distillation is no longer supplying any essential oil to the recipient, as it is precisely the presence of a certain quantity of oil in the water which up to this moment gave it a milky appearance.

Cordials.—In the preparation of cordials or liqueurs, scrupulous cleanliness is of the utmost consequence; and the best of sugar, the purest of rectified spirits, the best of herbs or essences, and distilled or filtered rain-water should be used. Where possible, distillation should nearly always be employed in the preparation of liqueurs, lemon and orange liqueurs being perhaps exceptions. If, however, distillation is impracticable, prolonged maceration for a month or more should be resorted to. In this case, in adapting the recipes in this chapter, only enough water is to be employed to make up the total to the amount ordered to be distilled off. If, instead of the herbs or spices themselves, it is decided to use the prepared essences, care should be taken to obtain essences prepared from the herbs, and not mere

STILL-ROOM OF THE LONDON ESSENCE CO.

chemical imitations.   Messrs. Bush, Messrs. Stafford,

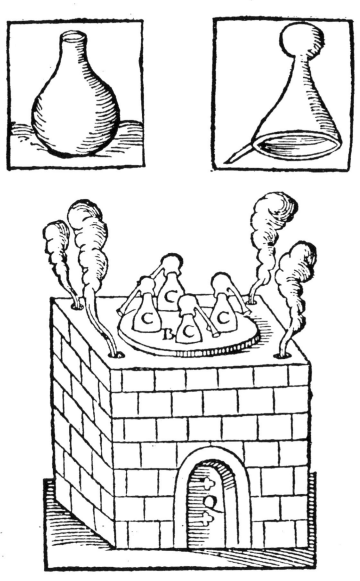

FURNACE WITH STILLS.

(From Peter Morwyng's "Treasure of Enonymus," 1559.)

Allen & Co., and the London Essence Co. may be communicated with.   The syrup is always added to the distillate last of all, and should have been carefully filtered through a clean filter-bag. If care be taken, the liqueur will be clear as soon as made, or at any rate after standing for a few days. Should, however, this not be the case, the liquid may be fined with whites of eggs, allowing one egg to three gallons. In any case, the liqueur should be stored

PERSIAN ROSE-WATER SPRINKLER.

for some months—preferably for a year or more—before being used.

The following are recipes for the making of a number of cordials by distillation. Those who wish to pursue the subject further may be referred to an admirable series of articles which appeared in the *Mineral Water Trade Review* from September, 1902, to May, 1903.

To make Absinthe.—Digest for a week, in a closed

vessel, a mixture of one gallon of rectified spirit, half a gallon of water, two pounds of wormwood tops, and eight grains each of dittany leaves, aniseed, calamus root, and angelica root. Add another half-gallon of water, and distil off six quarts at a moderate heat. Add a pint of syrup containing one pound of sugar.

A PERFORATED WATER-BATH.

A PORTABLE COPPER STILL.

To make Aniseed Cordial.—Proceed as for clove cordial, substituting half a pound of bruised aniseed and two ounces each of fennel and coriander seeds for the cloves and allspice, and drawing off only six quarts.

To make Benedictine.—Digest for a week, in a closed vessel, a mixture of a gallon of rectified spirits, a gallon of water, two ounces of cardamoms, an ounce each of balm, peppermint, genepi, and angelica root, half an ounce of calamus, a dram of cinnamon, and half a dram each of cloves and nutmeg. Distil off a gallon, and add syrup (made by dissolving eight pounds of sugar in three quarts of water) and three quarts of water.

To make Green Chartreuse.—Digest for a week, in a closed vessel, a mixture of a gallon of rectified spirits, a gallon of water, an ounce and a half of lemon-peel, an ounce of balm, half an ounce each of dried peppermint, mountain wormwood, and dried hyssop flowers, three drams of angelica root, a dram of calamus root, half a dram each of cloves, cinnamon, and mace, and a quarter of a dram of cardamoms. Distil off one gallon, and add syrup (made by heating five pounds of sugar in two quarts of water) and a pint of water, colouring the liqueur with a spirituous infusion of spinach or parsley.

To make Cinnamon Cordial.—Proceed as for clove cordial, substituting half a pound of cinnamon or cassia bark for the cloves and allspice, and distilling at a somewhat lower temperature.

To make Clove Cordial.—Digest for a week, in a closed vessel kept moderately warm, a mixture of one gallon of rectified spirits, one gallon of water, one ounce of bruised cloves, and one dram of allspice. Place the mixture in the still, and draw off six and a half quarts at a moderate heat. Sweeten with syrup (made by heating five pounds

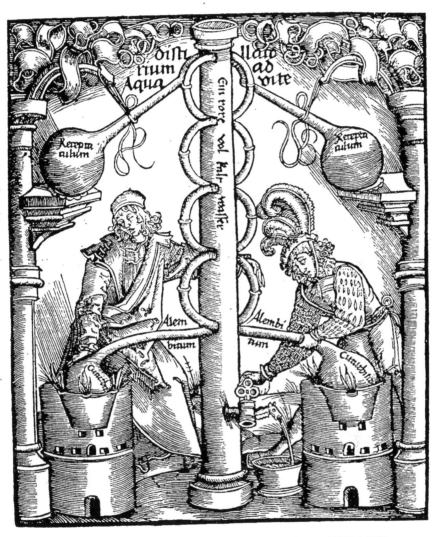

OLD APPARATUS USED FOR CONDENSING THE DISTILLATE.

(From the title-page of the second volume of Brunschwig's "Liber de Arte Distillandi," 1507.)

of sugar with two quarts of water, and skimming), and colour with cochineal.

To make Hamburgh Bitters.—Digest for a week, in a closed vessel, a mixture of a gallon of rectified spirits, a gallon of water, two ounces of cinnamon, one ounce each of wormwood, quassia, calamus root, and centaury, half an ounce each of aniseed, orris, coriander, and cloves, and a dram each of ginger, cardamoms, and mace. Distil off one gallon, and add syrup (made by heating three pounds of sugar in three pints of water) and three pints of water.

To make Kirschenwasser.—Digest for a week, in a closed vessel, a mixture of a gallon of rectified spirits, half a gallon of water, a pound of crushed cherry stones, half a pound of crushed apricot stones, an ounce of dried peach leaves, and two drams of myrrh. Distil off a gallon, and add three pints of spirit of noyau (made by distilling off three pints from a digested mixture of three pints of rectified spirits, a pint and half of water, and a pound of bruised apricot stones), a pint of orange-flower water, a gallon and a half of rectified spirits, syrup (made by heating thirty pounds of sugar in three gallons of water), and water to make up to eight and a half gallons.

To make Kummel.—Digest for a week, in a closed vessel, a mixture of a gallon of rectified spirits, a gallon of water, half a pound of caraway-seeds, three drams of orris root, and an ounce of fennel seeds.

"Beholde here a manner or fashion of Balneo Mariæ, verye excellent, of which the vessell large and greate is of tynne ; the bottome or bellye of the same standing wythin the boyling water. On thys great vessell is Lymbeck of Tynne, covered and compassed of another vessell like of Tynne farre larger."

(From Baker's " The Newe Jewell of Health," 1576.)

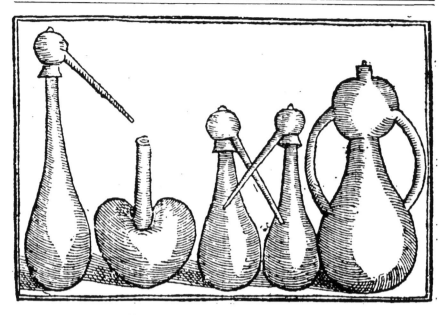

OLD VESSELS USED IN DISTILLING.

(From Baker's " Jewell of Health," 1576.)

TENDING THE FURNACE.

(From Baker's "Jewell of Health," 1576.)

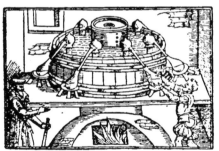

BALNEUM MARIÆ.

(From Baker's " Jewell of Health," 1576.)

Distil off one gallon, and add syrup (made by heating seven and a half pounds of sugar in three quarts of water) and a quart of water.

To make Lemon Cordial.—Proceed as for cinnamon cordial, substituting three-quarters of a pound of dried lemon-peel for the cinnamon.

To make Noyau.—Digest for a week, in a closed vessel, a mixture of a gallon of rectified spirits, a gallon of water, two pounds of crushed apricot or peach stones, and one pound of crushed plum or prune stones. Distil off five quarts, and add a gallon of syrup containing eight pounds of sugar and a gallon of water.

To make Orange Cordial.—Proceed as for cinnamon cordial, substituting three-quarters of a pound of the yellow part of fresh orange-peel for the cinnamon.

SOME OTHER CORDIALS AND BITTERS.

" There is no nation yet known in either hemisphere where the people of all conditions are more in want of some cordial to keep up their spirits than in this of ours."—SWIFT.

THE following recipes are for the making of cordials by simple mixing without distillation. Nearly all require straining, and some may require to be filtered through filter-paper.

To make Angostura Bitters.—Digest for a month, in a covered vessel, a mixture of a gallon of rectified spirits, a gallon and a half of water, two ounces of orange-peel, an ounce and a quarter of angostura bark, three-quarters of an ounce each of alkanet root and red sanderswood, half an ounce of gentian root, two drams each of cardamoms, Turkey rhubarb, cinnamon, caraway, coriander, and wormwood, and fifteen grains of turmeric. Strain, and add a pound of honey. Filter, and bottle.

To make Balm of Molucca.—Digest for a month, in a covered vessel, a mixture of a gallon of rectified spirits, a gallon of water, an ounce of cloves, and two drams of mace. Filter, and add a gallon of syrup (containing eight pounds of sugar) and two quarts of water.

To make Brandy Shrub.—Digest for a month a

mixture of a gallon of brandy, the peel of two oranges and a lemon, a pint each of orange juice and lemon juice, and five pints of syrup (containing four pounds of sugar). Strain, and bottle.

To make Cassis.—Digest for a week, in a covered vessel, a mixture of a gallon of rectified spirits, half a gallon of water, two ounces of cinnamon, and sixteen bruised cloves. At the end of the week add a gallon of black currants, and digest for a further two months. Press and strain, and add half a gallon of syrup (containing eight pounds of sugar).

To make Cherry Brandy.—Digest for three months, in a closed vessel, a mixture of a gallon of good brandy and a gallon of fresh cherries, of which about one-quarter of the stones have been broken. Strain, and add two pounds of loaf sugar.

To make Crême de Cacao.—Mix a gallon of rectified spirits with six pints of water, two and a half pints of syrup (containing two and a half pounds of sugar), and six and a quarter ounces of Bush's essence of cocoa.

To make Crême de Cacao (another way).—Digest for a month, in a covered vessel, a gallon of rectified spirits, a quart of water, two pounds of caracca, roasted and bruised cocoa-nuts, a pound of West Indian cacao-nuts, and a shred of vanilla. Add a quart of syrup (containing two pounds of sugar). Strain, and bottle.

To make Crême de Café.—Digest for a month, in

a covered vessel, a gallon of rectified spirits, two pounds of coffee ground and roasted, and a gallon of water. Add two quarts of syrup (containing four pounds of sugar). Strain, and bottle.

To make Crême de Menthe.—Mix five quarts of rectified spirits, a quarter of an ounce of oil of peppermint, two gallons of syrup (containing sixteen pounds of sugar) and half a pint of glycerine. Colour as with green chartreuse.

To make Curaçoa.—Digest for a month, in a covered vessel, a mixture of the peel of nine Seville oranges, the peel of a lemon, a dram each of cinnamon, coriander, and mace, an ounce of bruised Brazil wood, and a pint of rectified spirits. This tincture, having been filtered, is used to flavour a mixture of a gallon of rectified spirits, a gallon of water, and a gallon of syrup (containing eight pounds of sugar).

To make Ginger Brandy.—Digest for a month, in a covered vessel, stirring daily, a mixture of a gallon of brandy, six pounds of sugar, two pounds of raisins, half a pound of sweet almonds, two ounces each of bitter almonds and crushed ginger, an ounce of caraway seeds, and six lemons cut into slices.

To make Lemon Brandy.—Proceed as with cherry brandy, substituting a dozen sliced lemons for the cherries, and adding one pound of sugar only.

To make Lemon Cordial.—Digest for a month or more, in a closed vessel, a mixture of a gallon of rectified spirits, half a pound of lemon-peel, quarter of a pound of orange-peel, half an ounce of cinnamon, half an ounce of coriander, and five pints of

COPPER SPIRIT-MEASURE.

water. Strain, and add six pints of syrup (containing six pounds of sugar) and three quarts of water.

To make Orange Bitters.—Digest for a month, in a closed vessel, a mixture of a gallon of rectified spirits, a gallon of water, a pound of dried orange-peel, half a pound of gentian root, two ounces each of coriander and cinnamon, and an ounce of cardamoms. Strain, and add five pints of syrup (containing five pounds of sugar) and two quarts of water.

COPPER FUNNEL.

To make Rum Shrub. — As brandy shrub, substituting rum for brandy.

To make Sighs of Love.—Mix a gallon of rectified

spirits, two gallons of syrup (containing twelve pounds of sugar), water six pints, eau de rose one quart, and four drops of essence of vanilla. Colour delicately with cochineal.

To make Sloe Gin.—Digest for a year a mixture of a gallon of unpricked sloes, a gallon of gin, and six or eight pounds of sugar.

To make Tent.—Digest a mixture of a quart of port, a pint of sherry, a pint of rectified spirits, a quarter of a pint each of lemon juice and orange-flower water, three and a half pints of syrup (containing two pounds of sugar), and three drops of essence of ambergris.

To make Usquebaugh.—Digest for a month, in a covered vessel, shaking daily, a mixture of a gallon of brandy, a pound of stoned raisins, a pound of sugar candy, an ounce each of crushed cinnamon, cloves, cardamoms, caraways, and nutmeg, a quarter ounce of saffron, and the rind of a Seville orange.

To make Vermouth.—Digest for a month, in a closed vessel, a quart of rectified spirits, two and a half gallons of a white wine, a sliced orange, two bruised nutmegs, half an ounce each of centaury, germander, calamus, elecampane, wormwood, and blessed thistle, and a quarter of an ounce each of gentian root and angelica root. Filter, and bottle.

"Life isn't all beer and skittles—but beer and skittles, or something better of the same sort, must form a good part of every Englishman's education."—TOM HUGHES.

*T*O *make Ale Cup.*—Digest for a few hours (preferably for a few days) a quarter of an ounce each of cinnamon and allspice and a couple of cloves in a tea-cupful of sherry, and strain through muslin. Add to this infusion four bottles of ginger beer and a quart of ale. Cool on ice, and serve in tankards.

To make Badminton.—Mix in a jug, placed on ice, a bottle of soda-water, a bottle of claret, a glass of sherry, a glass of maraschino, the peel and juice of a lemon, a table-spoonful of castor sugar, and a sprig of borage.

To make Bishop.—Stick four Seville oranges with cloves, and roast them brown before the fire. Place the oranges in a covered earthenware vessel before the fire, together with half a pound of castor sugar, a quarter of an ounce of mixed ginger, nutmeg, and cinnamon, and half a pint each of water and of claret. Let it stand for a few hours—preferably for twenty-four hours. Then squeeze the oranges, and strain. Warm the mixture and add a boiling mixture of half a pint of claret and a quarter of a pint of port.

" Fine oranges,
Well roasted, with sugar and wine in a cup,
They'll make a sweet Bishop when gentlefolks sup."

117

To make Boston Cooler.—Place in a tumbler a bottle of sarsaparilla, a bottle of ginger ale, the rind of a lemon thinly sliced, and a few bits of ice.

The best way to break a piece of ice into smaller pieces is to use a large needle and strike it with a hammer; or it may be crushed by wrapping it in a napkin or other cloth and hitting it with a mallet.

To make a Brandy Cocktail.—Fill a tumbler with chipped ice, and pour thereon three drops of Boker's or angostura bitters, six drops of syrup, and half a wine-glassful of brandy. Stir for a minute, and then strain into a wine-glass containing either a small piece of lemon-peel or a few drops of curaçoa.

To make Champagne Cobbler.—Half fill a large tumbler with shaved ice, add the juice of half a lemon and a tea-spoonful of soda, and fill up with champagne. Dash a little claret over the top. This should be served with straws.

To make Champagne Cup.—Mix in a jug, placed on ice, a bottle of champagne, two bottles of soda-water, a liqueur-glassful of brandy, a liqueur-glassful of curaçoa or maraschino, two table-spoonfuls of sugar, a thin slice of cucumber (which remove before serving), a pound of ice, and a sprig of verbena.

To make Cider Cup.—Proceed as with champagne cup, replacing the champagne by cider, and using only one bottle of soda-water.

Simple Claret Cup.—Extract the "zest" or

essential oil from the peel of a lemon by rubbing four lumps of sugar upon it. Pare another lemon as thinly as you can. Put the paring and the sugar into a large jug, and pour in a quart of claret. Mix all well together, and set the jug on ice for one hour. Just before serving add a pint of sparkling moselle and two bottles of soda-water. Put a few sprigs of borage or of balm into the jug.—*J. R.*

To make Coffee.—Purchase whole, and preferably unroasted, berries of good quality from a reliable source. Roast freshly as required, grind as soon as roasted, and make as soon as ground. Some admirably simple coffee-roasters are now obtainable. In the absence of a proper roaster, a frying-pan may be used, a few berries being roasted at a time. A very little butter should be placed in the pan, a low fire should be employed, and the berries should be kept on the move till they are of a light brown colour. It should be remembered that a single burnt berry will spoil the coffee. Coffee should be most carefully strained, and therefore some form of coffee-pot with percolator is desirable. Pack the freshly ground coffee tightly in the strainer, and slowly pour boiling water on it. As soon as the coffee has percolated through, it should be served. Boiling it drives off the aroma. A table-spoonful of ground coffee should be allowed to each *café noir* cup, or each large cup of *café au lait*. *Café au lait* consists of an equal mixture of coffee and boiled milk.

To make Crambambuli.—Boil half a pound of sugar in a quart of ale. Beat six eggs with half a pint of cold ale. Add the boiling ale, and serve.

To make an Egg-and-Brandy Mixture.—Beat up the yolks of two eggs. Thoroughly mix with a tea-cupful each of brandy and cinnamon water.

To make Egg Flip. (From "Oxford Night-Caps.") —Egg posset, *alias* egg flip, otherwise, in college language, rum booze. Beat up well the yolks of eight eggs with refined sugar pulverized, and a nutmeg grated ; then extract the juice from the rind of a lemon by rubbing loaf sugar upon it, and put the sugar, with a piece of cinnamon and a quart of strong home-brewed beer, into a saucepan, place it on the fire, and when it boils take it off, then add a single glass of gin, or this may be left out, put the liquor into a spouted jug, and pour it gradually among the yolks of eggs, etc. All must be kept well stirred with a spoon while the liquor is being poured in. If it be not sweet enough, add loaf sugar.

To make Egg Nog.—Well beat the yolks of six eggs, and mix them with half a pound of castor sugar, stirring till the sugar is dissolved. Add this to a mixture of a pint of brandy, a pint of rum, and three pints of milk, stirring the while. Pour over the whole the well-beaten whites of six eggs, and lastly grate a little nutmeg over all. Having been cooled over ice, this should be served in small tumblers. If hot egg nog is desired, use hot milk.

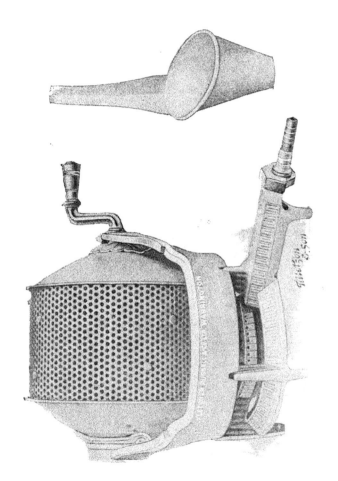

A SIMPLE COFFEE ROASTER

Fruit Drink.—Mash one pint of strawberries, raspberries, currants, or mulberries in a pint of water, into which the juice of two lemons has been squeezed. Add a little sifted sugar. Strain through a hair sieve. If not sufficiently liquid, add some iced water or half a bottle of soda-water.—*J. R.*

To make John Collin's Gin Sling, or Gin Fizz.—Mix in a tumbler the juice of half a lemon, a small tea-spoonful of castor sugar, and a wine-glassful of Hollands or of Old Tom gin. Stir for two minutes, then add a few pieces of ice and a bottle of soda-water.

To make La Masubal, or Lamb's Wool.—Roast half a dozen apples, having previously cored them. Boil a small piece of crushed ginger, a quarter of a nutmeg grated, and two or three ounces of sugar in a quart of strong ale. Add the pulp of the roasted apples, and serve hot.

Lemonade.—To make one quart of lemonade allow six ripe lemons, or eight if they are not juicy. Take four good-sized lumps of sugar and rub the outside of the lemons well with them, in order to extract the " zest " of the rind. Pick out every pip, and squeeze every drop of juice the lemons will yield into a jug. Then add the four lumps of sugar, and pour in nearly a quart of boiling water. Cover the jug till the lemonade is cold. It is an improvement to set the lemonade on ice, but do not put any pieces of ice into it.—*J. R.*

The Long Drink.—Take a large soda-water

tumbler, and bruise into it twelve or more straw-berries, or any fruit which will yield not less than a table-spoonful of juice. Add a table-spoonful of cream, and fill up with soda-water.—*J. R.*

To make Mint Julep.—Place four or five sprigs of mint in a tumbler, together with a table-spoonful of castor sugar and two table-spoonfuls of water. Stir for two minutes, then add a wine-glassful of brandy,

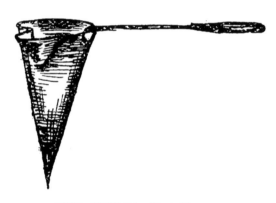

BEER WARMER OR MULLER.

and fill up the tumbler with shaved ice. The lip of the tumbler may be rubbed with a piece of fresh pine-apple.

> " *Behold this cordial Julep here*
> *That foams and dances in his crystal bounds,*
> *With spirits of balm and fragrant spices mix'd.*"

To make Mulled Ale.—Boil a quart of ale with a table-spoonful of sugar, a tea-spoonful of crushed ginger, and two or three cloves. Beat up eight eggs in a quarter of a pint of cold ale, and place in a large jug. Pour the boiling ale on this mixture, and then pour the resultant to and from another jug for some minutes in such a way as to froth the mixture fully.

Mulled Claret.—Put half a pint of claret into a saucepan with a little water, six or eight cloves, and a piece of cinnamon. Make it boiling hot. Grate a little nutmeg and a little ground ginger very finely into a jug, pour the claret in, and add a lump of sugar which has been well rubbed on the rind of a lemon.—*J. R.*

To make Hot Milk Punch.—Dissolve half a pound of sugar in a quart of boiling milk. Add half a bottle of brandy and a quarter of a bottle of rum, grating a little nutmeg over the surface, and adding the thin outer rind and juice of four lemons.

To make Milk Punch for Bottling.—Place the thin outer peel and the juice of three Seville oranges and three lemons, with half a nutmeg grated, in a bottle with a pint of brandy, and leave it to stand for a few days. Then add a quart of brandy, a pint of rum, a pound of sugar, and three pints of water. Add a quart of boiling milk, and stir thoroughly. Let the mixture stand for twenty-four hours, and then strain through muslin, and bottle.

To make Hot English Punch.—Rub twelve or more lumps of sugar over the rind of four lemons until the yellow part has been removed. Throw the sugar into the jug or bowl, and make up the weight of sugar to a pound. Add the juice of the lemons and two quarts of boiling water, and stir for five minutes. Then add a bottle of brandy and half a bottle of rum.

To make Cold Punch.—Proceed as with hot punch, but replacing the boiling water by cold water and a few pieces of ice. The punch itself is better not cooled over ice before serving.

To make Cold Gin Punch.—Rub a few lumps of sugar over the outer peel of a lemon, and place this, with the juice of the lemon, in a jug or bowl, together with enough sugar to make up to three ounces. Add half a pint of gin, a wine-glassful of maraschino, a pint of water, and two bottles of iced soda-water.

To make Purl.—Beat three eggs to a froth, and well mix them with two ounces of castor sugar and a gill of ale. Heat a quart of ale with a tea-spoonful of powdered nutmeg and a table-spoonful of crushed ginger. Slowly add the hot ale to the ale-and-eggs mixture. Lastly, add a wine-glassful of gin or brandy.

" For the rest, both the tap and the parlour of the Six Jolly Fellowship Porters gave upon the river, and had red curtains matching the noses of the regular customers, and were provided with comfortable fireside utensils, like models of sugar-loaf hats, made in that shape that they might, with their pointed ends, seek out for themselves glowing nooks in the depths, where they mulled your ale, or heated for you those delectable drinks —purls, flip, and dog's nose. The first of these humming compounds was a specialty of The Porters, which,

through an inscription on its door-posts, gently appealed to your feelings as ' The Early Purl House.' "

To make Raspberry Vinegar.—Pour two quarts of best vinegar over one quart of raspberries picked from their stalks but not mashed. Leave them for twenty-four hours. Next day put the vinegar and fruit on the fire till it just boils, and then squeeze it through a cloth. Add two pounds of sugar, and let all simmer for ten minutes. This quantity makes six bottles. A gill of raspberry vinegar mixed into a tumbler of seltzer water makes a most refreshing drink.—*J. R.*

To make Raspberry Vinegar (another recipe).—Take a quart of raspberries and place them in a jar. Cover them with a pint of vinegar. In three days pour off the vinegar, and replace the raspberries by a fresh lot, again pouring the vinegar over them. In three days pour off the vinegar again, strain it, add a pound of sugar, boil for five minutes, skim it, and bottle it.

To make Saratoga Cobbler.—Half fill a tumbler with shaved ice, and place therewith a liqueur-glassful each of brandy, whisky, and vermouth, and four drops of angostura bitters. Mix thoroughly, strain, and add a slice of lemon.

To make Shandy Gaff.—Pour into a tumbler coincidently equal quantities of beer and ginger beer.

To make Sherbet.—Dry separately a pound of fine castor sugar, half a pound of carbonate of soda, and half a pound of tartaric acid. Add to the sugar a large tea-spoonful of essence of lemon, then add the acid and soda, and well mix. The sherbet should at once be securely bottled, as the least damp destroys its virtue.

To make Sherry Cobbler.—Half fill a tumbler with shaved ice. Add two wine-glassfuls of sherry and a table-spoonful of castor sugar. Stir. This should be served with straws.

To make a Syllabub.—Place in a large basin half a pint of sherry and three ounces of castor sugar. Dissolve the sugar, and then add to the mixture a pint of warm milk slowly poured from a height so as to make a froth.

To make Tewahdiddle.—"This is a right gossip's cup, that far exceeds all the ale that ever Mother Bunch made in her lifetime." To half a pint of beer add a dessert-spoonful of brandy, half a tea-spoonful of brown sugar, a slice of lemon and some nutmeg grated. It may be drunk cold, or the beer may be heated before mixing.

To make a bowl of Wassail.—"*At night to sup, and then to cards, and last of all, to have a flaggon of ale and apples, drunk out of a wood cup, as a Christmas draught, which made all merry.*" Boil a quarter of an ounce each of bruised ginger, cinnamon, nutmeg, and a couple each of cloves, corianders, and cardamoms in three-quarters of a tumblerful of water for ten minutes. Add a quart of ale, a bottle of sherry, and from half a pound to a pound of sugar. Heat, but do not get too near the boiling-point. Then beat the yolks of six eggs and the whites of three eggs, and throw them into the bowl. Slowly add half the heated ale and wine, stirring all the while. Bring the remainder to the boil and pour it also in the bowl. Lastly, throw into the bowl six roasted apples which had been cored and stuffed with sugar and think of Puck's confession—

> "Sometimes lurk I in a gossip's bowl,
> In very likeness of a roasted crab,
> And, when she drinks, against her lips I bob,
> And in her wither'd dewlaps pour the ale!"

HINTS FOR REFRESHMENTS AT A GARDEN-PARTY OR PICNIC

IT may be useful to give a general idea of the quantities required in providing for a party of, say, eighty guests.

Five gallons of tea, allowing five ounces of good tea to each gallon. Six gallons of coffee, half to be served hot with milk, and half to be served iced, allowing eight ounces of coffee to each gallon. Three gallons of claret-cup, allowing for each gallon four bottles of claret and four bottles of soda-water. Twelve quarts of water-ice; six quarts to be of lemon ice and six of strawberry ice. Twelve dishes of sandwiches, of different kinds; these are sure to be popular, and a tolerable supply should be kept in reserve. Four dishes of rolled brown bread and butter, and the same quantity of white. Eight pounds of plum-cake cut up into small thick pieces. Six pounds of freshly made sponge finger biscuits. Two or more bowls of *macédoine* of fruit. Oat-cake cut into long fingers and spread with Devonshire cream is popular, and so are small scones split open and filled with Devonshire cream. A few kinds of sandwiches suitable for garden-parties may be mentioned here.

Salad Sandwiches.—Use watercress picked from the hard stems, mustard and cress, or shred lettuce leaves. Spread the bread with *maître d'hôtel* butter.

For this, add to two ounces of butter the juice of one lemon, a dessert-spoonful of chopped parsley leaf freed from all moisture, a pinch of white pepper, and a pinch of salt.

Cucumber Sandwiches.—Pare the cucumber, and just before the sandwiches are wanted cut it into very thin slices. Place the cucumber between thin pieces of white bread and butter stamped out with a round cutter.

Rolled Sandwiches.—Pound in a mortar two ounces of cooked tongue or ham freed from skin and fat, a quarter of a pound of cooked chicken or turkey, two table-spoonfuls of *maître d'hôtel* butter, one ounce of plain butter, and six table-spoonfuls of fine white of bread-crumbs. When the mixture is smooth, add a dust of pepper and a small pinch of salt, and pass it through a sieve. Sprinkle a few bread-crumbs lightly on a pastry-board, take a little of the mixture, and pat it out with a knife dipped in hot water. Make it two inches and a half long, and one inch and a half wide. Trim the edges, and raise it carefully from the board with the knife, rolling it over as you raise it. If the mixture is too moist add a few more bread-crumbs, but if it is too dry it will break and not roll. Dish the rolls on a bed or cress.

Green Sandwich Rolls.—Pound the yolk of a hard-boiled egg with a quarter of a pound of butter, six sprigs of watercress, and six sprigs of parsley. Blanch the watercress and parsley by throwing them for five minutes into boiling water. Press them dry in a cloth, but do not squeeze them. Then add a dust of pepper and salt, and six table-spoonfuls of brown bread-crumbs; and when the mixture is smooth roll it as in the former recipe.

Sweet Sandwiches can be made of any jam or marmalade. They are better without butter, and the preserve should be very lightly spread. They should be about four inches long and one inch wide. Chocolate, melted in a little hot milk, and spread between slices of stale sponge cake, makes a popular sandwich.

Macédoine of Fruit.—Put three lumps of sugar and the thinly pared rind of half a lemon into a quarter or a pint of water, and boil it for ten minutes. Then add, if possible, twelve raspberries. If raspberries cannot be had, add the juice of the half lemon. Let it boil up, skim it, and set it on ice till quite cold. Then add a dessert-spoonful of good brandy. Put into a china bowl currants freed from their stalks, raspberries and strawberries picked from their stems, peaches and apricots stoned and cut into quarters, black and white grapes, and a few mulberries. Crack the stones of the peaches and apricots, peel the kernels, and add them to the fruit in the bowl. Set the bowl on ice. Ten minutes before the *macédoine* is wanted, pour the cold syrup gently over the fruit, and keep the bowl on a dish filled with crushed ice. Help the *macédoine* with a soup-ladle instead of a spoon.

Travellers' Sandwiches. — These are so often coarsely and carelessly made that the traveller on whom the sandwiches are bestowed flies in disgust to the dainties of the railway refreshment-room.

SOME OLD MORTARS.

Sandwiches should be packed in the paper known as "butter paper," and if they have to be cut some time before they are wanted, they should be kept under a damp cloth, as they soon become dry if covered with a dish. A small leaf of young lettuce, or a little cress, improves most sandwiches.

Ham Sandwiches.—Work a little mustard into

the butter you mean to use, and butter both the slices of bread on one side. Lay a thin slice of ham between the pieces of buttered bread, and press the sandwiches under a light weight.

Beef Sandwiches.—Prepare these in the same way, but add a little grated horseradish to the butter as well as the mustard.

Chicken Sandwiches.—Use slices of chicken and ham, or chicken and tongue, or pound the two together. Spread a little *maître d'hôtel* butter on the bread.

Gladstone Sandwiches.—Use crisp toast instead of bread, butter the toast with *maître d'hôtel* butter, and cover it with finely shred celery. Cold game is best for these sandwiches.

Travellers' Rolls.—Make dinner rolls the size and shape of an egg, scoop out part of the crumb, and fill the space with pounded cooked meat moistened with *maître d'hôtel* butter, and well mixed with shred lettuce, mustard and cress, or sliced cucumber.

Egg Sandwiches.—Put some fresh eggs into water which is already boiling fast, and let them boil for fifteen minutes. Peel off the shells, cut the eggs into slices lengthwise (not across, or the yolk and white will not be equally divided), and place them between slices of bread and butter. Mix both salt and pepper into the butter before you spread it. Or pound the eggs when they are cold and shelled, pounding the white and the yolk together in a mortar. Add a little butter, salt, pepper, and a dust of cayenne, and spread the mixture on thin slices of bread.

Cheese and Celery Sandwiches.—Mix freshly grated cheese with an ounce of butter till it becomes a thick paste. Spread this on thin slices of bread, and cover it with celery shred as finely as possible.

Beef Roll.—This is excellent for a journey if cut into sandwiches.

Mince very finely one pound of raw beefsteak and a quarter of a pound of cooked ham. The meat should be passed twice through the mincing machine. Add to the meat one well-beaten egg and two ounces of dried and sifted bread-crumbs. Season with pepper and salt, but be careful not to put too much. Then mix all well together with a wooden spoon. Shape the meat into a roll, and tie it up in a cloth, fastening the ends tightly. Boil the roll for three hours, and glaze it. When cut up into sandwiches, the mustard spread on the meat should be mixed with water in which a little horse-radish has been grated.

Out-of-Door Meals.—A good way of packing a light summer luncheon is to take two strong biscuit-tins of the two-pound size, then to line them with lettuce leaves at the bottom and sides, and finally to arrange packets of sandwiches in one tin, with more lettuce to cover them. In the other tin set a loaf of bread and a plain luncheon cake, with a good clasp knife, and pack the space left with fruit and whole tomatoes. Bottles of cold tea should be taken in another basket, with a bottle or two of claret or light beer, and a few tumblers. For a boating-trip lasting a day or two the following suggestions may be found useful. When you encamp by the riverside, and your fire is burning, put on the saucepan with ten potatoes roughly peeled, three unpeeled onions, and a couple of carrots sliced. Pour in just enough water to cover the vegetables, and boil them for twenty minutes, keeping the lid of the saucepan tightly closed. After twenty minutes pour off the water, and put into the saucepan the contents of a one-pound tin of haricot-mutton, or beef, or Irish stew, and stir in two large spoonfuls of Bovril or Liebig's Essence of Meat. If Worcester sauce is liked, add a tea-spoonful of that. Stir all well together, and continue to stir the stew over a hot fire for five or six minutes. This makes a good dinner for two hungry men. If you can buy from a neighbouring garden some young potatoes and carrots use twenty of each. Do not peel the potatoes, only wash them and rub them with a coarse cloth. In washing up after such a meal use absolutely boiling water, for merely *hot* water is of no use. Fill your saucepan or cooking-pot with water, and when it boils scour it round a few times with a piece of house-flannel tied firmly to a stick. Do the same to the frying-pan. Put metal cups and plates into boiling water, also the blades of knives and the prongs of forks (keeping the handles out of the water). In this way they will soon be quite clean, and after a final dip in the river, and a rub with a dry cloth, they will shine like silver. If a bit of bacon can be procured do not fry it, but toast it on a toasting-fork before a clear part of the fire. The rashers of bacon should be cut thin, and they will be sufficiently toasted when the fat looks transparent. A gingerbread loaf, made according to the following family recipe, is useful for boating-trips, as the longer it lasts the better it is. Two pounds of brown flour, two pounds of treacle, a quarter of a pound of brown sugar, a breakfast-cupful of cream, two eggs, a tea-spoonful of carbonate of soda dissolved in a little hot water, two ounces and a half of ground ginger, and a little chopped citron. Mix all well together, and bake in a moderately hot oven.

Cold Tea.—Cold tea, properly made, is much appreciated on journeys, and is generally liked by shooting-parties on hot days. But good cold tea cannot be made by filling bottles with the remains of the tea at breakfast. Cold tea should be drunk unsweetened, and- if carelessly made it is flat and unpalatable. Wide-mouthed glass bottles with screw-tops, such as are sold for jam, are the best to use. Cold tea should be made from the best tea and freshly boiling water ; it should stand four minutes only, and should then be poured into the bottles through a tin strainer. A couple of lemons and a sharp clasp-knife should be packed in the basket with the bottles of tea, and a little metal box of sugar can be added for those who like it.

Iced Coffee.—Make strong coffee from freshly ground berries, add cold milk and a little sifted sugar. Put the coffee into glass jugs, and set these on ice for at least two hours before use. If pieces of ice are put into the coffee the flavour is spoilt.

Water Biscuits. Family Recipes.—(1) One pound of fine flour and two ounces of butter well rubbed together. Add a pinch of salt. Mix with cold water to a very stiff paste, and beat it well with a rolling-pin. Break the paste into pieces the size of a walnut, and roll each into a round. Prick each biscuit with a biscuit-pricker. Put them on a very hot baking-sheet, and bake in a very quick oven.

(2) Rub an ounce of butter into a handful of fine flour. Make it into a stiff, smooth paste with warm milk and the white of an egg beaten to a froth. Beat the paste with a rolling-pin for half an hour or longer, for the delicacy of the biscuits depends upon the length of time they are beaten. Then take small pieces of the paste and roll them out to the size of a saucer. They must be so thin as to be almost transparent. Bake the biscuits very lightly.

Water biscuits are often liked at dinner instead of bread or toast.

VERY good small refrigerators may now be bought, and are very useful both for the manufacture of ice and of ice creams, as well as for freezing puddings or cooling drinks. The following recipes are for a few of the more popular ice creams.

To make Strawberry Ice Cream.—To three-quarters of a pound of strawberries add half a pound of sugar (or a pound of strawberry jam may be used instead of fruit and sugar), and rub through a hair sieve. Add a pint of rich cream, and very little cochineal. Well mix, and freeze. Raspberry ice cream may be made in the same way.

To make Vanilla Ice Cream.—Make a custard with the yolks of five eggs and a pint of milk, and add two ounces of castor sugar and a little vanilla. Cool, and partly freeze. Then add and well mix half a pint of cream, and freeze.

To make Maraschino Ice Cream.—Mix a pint of cream, a quarter of a pound of castor sugar, the juice of half a lemon, and two wine-glassfuls of maraschino, and freeze.

To make Coffee Ice Cream.—Mix half a pint of very strong, good coffee with the yolks of six eggs, six ounces of castor sugar, and a pint of cream, and freeze.

To make Lemon Ice Cream.—Rub castor sugar over the rind of two lemons, making the sugar up to six ounces. Mix this sugar with the juice of the lemons and a pint of cream, and freeze.

I T may not be out of place to give a few well-tried recipes for the benefit of invalids.

Beef-tea.—Procure beef which has been freshly killed. Take one pound of beef free from the least particle of fat, gristle, sinew, or skin. Mince it with a knife, not with a machine. Put the beef into one pint of cold water, and stir for ten minutes. Bring it to the boil, and boil it for half an hour, never ceasing to stir it. Strain, and add a dust of salt only. Serve with strips of dry toast, and salt in a salt-cellar.

Cold Beef-tea.—This can be digested by persons who cannot take the usual beef-tea. Mince one pound of raw beef as finely as possible. Pour upon it one quart of boiling water. Plunge the jar in a deep saucepan ready filled with boiling water. Set it near the fire, but not so close as to make it simmer. Draw the saucepan gradually away from the fire, and let the beef-tea get nearly cold. Then strain it through muslin, and after that filter it through clean white blotting-paper. Serve cold.

Chicken Broth.—Roast a chicken for fifteen minutes, not longer. Cut it into slices, and put it into a saucepan with three pints of cold water. Season very lightly with pepper and salt. Bring it gradually to the boil, and let it simmer very gently. An old fowl will take from four to six hours, a

young one will need three hours. Strain, and take
off every particle of fat. The previous roasting of
the chicken is a great improvement. If the broth
is liked thick, simmer in it two ounces of crushed
tapioca or sago.

Nourishing Broth.—Make the chicken broth as in
the foregoing recipe, but when the chicken is put
into the saucepan to simmer, add to it two pounds
of fresh shin of beef, without fat, and cook the
chicken and beef together. Or, if the chicken
cannot be had, use a knuckle of veal. Put the beef
and veal into five quarts of cold water. Add a
little salt, bring the broth to the boil, and simmer
slowly. The beef and veal must be simmered in
five quarts of water till this is gradually reduced to
three pints of broth. Strain, and remove any fat.

Chicken Food for an Invalid.—Take a good
chicken and remove all the white meat. Cut up
the remainder into small pieces, and stew it in a
quart of water till it is reduced one-third. Let it
cool. Then remove every particle of fat or grease.
Put in the white meat of the chicken, and simmer
gently for fifteen minutes. Then pound it to a
paste in a mortar. Return the pounded meat to
the broth, and again simmer as gently as possible
for fifteen minutes more. Season with just a dust
of pepper and salt, and serve cold in a small mould.

Mutton Cutlet for an Invalid.—Take three of the
nicest cutlets from the best part of a neck of
mutton. Trim one cutlet very neatly, and trim

the other two so that when placed together the outer cutlets will project beyond the middle one. Tie the three together, the cutlet intended for the invalid being in the centre. Turn all three with cutlet-tongs over and over till they are done. All the gravy will be concentrated in the middle cutlet. Send this to the invalid on a hot-water plate, and use the other cutlets in the dining-room.

Savoury Custard for an Invalid.—Take two eggs, using both whites and both yolks, and the yolks only of two more eggs. Beat them well with one gill of clear beef-tea, but do not add any salt. Put the custard into a well-buttered basin, cover the top with a buttered paper, set the basin in a pan of boiling water, and let it steam slowly. It will take about fifteen minutes. Let the custard get quite cold, then turn it out and cut it into diamonds with a cutter. Serve salt and pepper with the custard.

The Invalid's Yorkshire Pudding.—Mix the yolks of two eggs into two good table-spoonfuls of flour. Beat the whites of the eggs lightly, and stir all together. Bake for ten minutes in rather a quick oven.

Restorative Jelly.—Take two ounces of isinglass [in these days gelatine must be used], two ounces of white sugar candy, and half an ounce of gum arabic, grated. Steep these ingredients in a pint or port wine poured over them in an earthenware jar. Let it stand twelve hours. Put the jar in a saucepan of cold water, and let the water get gradually warm. Then simmer as slowly as possible, and continue simmering till the isinglass or gelatine is quite melted. The jelly will be thick. Do not strain it, but break up a table-spoonful at a time for use.

Rice Jelly.—Well wash half a pound of Carolina rice and boil it with a strip of lemon-peel for one hour in two quarts of water. Pass it through a sieve, and let it cool. When cold it will be a firm jelly. Add one pint of milk to the rice jelly, and boil all together till the rice resembles thickened milk. Stir constantly with a wooden spoon. Strain it, sweeten it a little, and serve warm.

Calves'-foot Jelly.—This is much better when the "set" of feet is prepared at home and not sent in ready for use by the butcher. First wash each foot separately and very thoroughly, then scald each in boiling water, and scrape off all the hair. Remove any fat from the clefts of the hoof. Put the feet into a stone jar, cover them with one gallon of cold water, bring it to the boil, and then either let it simmer for six hours or tie stout brown paper over the jar, and put it into the oven for three hours. Then strain the jelly through a sieve into an earthenware bowl. Let it get cold, then take off the fat at the top. Break up the jelly, being careful not to touch the sediment at the bottom of the bowl. The four feet ought to yield about two quarts of jelly. Do not clear the jelly, but add a little lemon juice as flavouring. Some invalids like a little of this jelly warmed as broth ; in this case omit the lemon-peel, and use as flavouring a tea-spoonful of thyme leaves finely minced and sewn up in a bit of muslin, removing the muslin before the jelly is strained.

Clear Barley Water.—Wash one pound of pearl barley very thoroughly, using fresh water two or three times. Put the barley into a quart jug with one lump of sugar. Fill the jug with boiling water, and let it stand to get cold. The barley will settle at the bottom, and the liquid will be clear. Pare the rind of a lemon as thinly as possible, put it into a breakfast-cup, pour boiling water upon it, and let it stand half an hour. Strain the liquid, put it into a glass jug, pour the barley water upon it, and set the jug on ice before serving.

Toast and Water.—This refreshing and nutritious drink must be freshly made, as it soon turns sour. Toast a thin slice of bread very slowly and carefully till it becomes very hard and brown, but not scorched or blackened. Put it into a jug, and pour upon it one quart of freshly drawn cold water. Cover the jug, and let the toast soak for one hour. Then take out the toast, and pour the water into the jug it is to be served in. Toast and water does not generally need straining, but it must be served quite cold.

American Crust Coffee.—Cut some thin slices of stale bread, and bake them in the oven till they are quite dark brown. Pound the slices in a mortar. Boil one ounce of bread-crumbs in half a pint of water, using a small saucepan. Take it off the fire, let it stand for a few minutes, and then strain the liquid through a fine tin strainer into a tumbler or breakfast-cup. Serve it hot. This is quite as nutritious as toast and water.

*T*O *make Sweet-Jar or Pot-Pourri.*—Take six pounds of bay-salt, beaten fine, twenty-four sweet-bay leaves, torn into strips, a handful of myrtle leaves, of the red part of clove carnations, of syringa or orange-blossom separated from the green calyx, of violets picked from their stalks, six handfuls of lavender blossoms, a handful of sweet verbena leaves, of thyme, of balm, of sweet marjoram, and of rosemary. Dry all these on a sheet spread in a sunny room. Then put them all into a large china jar, sprinkling the pounded bay-salt thoroughly amongst both flowers and leaves. In a short time they will become moist. Stir the contents of the jar well every day for a month, adding a little bay-salt occasionally. Keep the jar in the sun, closely covered with a china lid. When the pot-pourri has been in the jar for a day or two, add four ounces of orris root sliced, two ounces of beaten cloves, and the rinds of three Seville oranges and of three lemons finely pared, cut into strips, and well beaten. Cover the jar as before. Jessamine flowers, myrtle or syringa, or orange flowers, well dried in the sun, can be added at any time to the pot-pourri. Never adulterate pot-pourri by scents bought at a shop.— J. R.

To make Eau-de-Cologne.—Mix together a pint of rectified spirits, an ounce of orange-flower water, two drams of oil of bergamot, two drams of oil of lemon, twenty minims of oil of rosemary, and twenty minims of oil of neroli. Allow the mixture to stand for a couple of months, thoroughly shaking at intervals. Filter, if necessary.

To make Lavender Water without distillation.— Mix together a pint of rectified spirits, four ounces of distilled water, three drams of oil of lavender, three drams of orange-flower water, five minims each of oil of cloves and oil of cinnamon, and four minims of otto of roses. Allow this mixture to stand for a fortnight, then filter through carbonate of magnesia, and bottle. Keep for three months before using.

To make Aromatic Vinegar for Smelling Bottles.— Digest in a bottle for four days, with frequent shaking, a mixture of a pint of acetic acid (90 per cent.), one ounce each of dried lavender flowers, thyme, and rosemary, and twenty grains each of powdered cloves and cinnamon. Strain, filter through blotting-paper, and bottle.

To make Toilet Vinegar.—Mix an ounce of pure acetic acid with a pint of water, and digest therein, for two or three weeks, four ounces of fresh, or two ounces of dried, fragrant flowers or leaves. Among the best for the purpose are rose petals, lavender, elder blossom, rosemary, and thyme.

Scent Bags may be made with almost any dr fragrant leaves or flowers, such as the scented leaves of geraniums, lavender flowers, rose petals, and so on. These are tied up in linen bags, and placed in cushions, or suspended in wardrobes or cupboards. A good recipe is a pound of lavender flowers, two ounces of thyme, an ounce of ground cloves, and two ounces of salt. A more elaborate recipe is as follows : Grind into a coarsely powdered mixture a pound of orris root, a quarter of a pound each of rose

PERSIAN INCENSE BURNER.

petals, lavender flowers, and sandalwood shavings, two ounces of benzoin, a dram each of otto of roses and oil of cloves, a dram of musk, and half an ounce of vanilla pods.

To make Incense.—Coarsely powder and mix together a pound each of gum benzoin and frank-incense, a quarter of a pound each of cascarilla and gum myrrh, and half an ounce of cinnamon.

To make Aromatic or Fumigating Pastils.—Mix together the following ingredients, all having been separately powdered : two pounds of charcoal, one pound each of frankincense and gum benzoin, and half a pound of gum storax. Add to the mixed powders, four ounces of syrup, six ounces of tincture of benzoin, two ounces each of oil of almonds and essence of ambergris, and one ounce of essence of musk. Make the resultant paste into cones, adding a little warm water if required.

To make Aromatic Pastils. Another Recipe.—Mix together 125 parts of gum benzoin, 25 parts of balsam of tolu, 100 parts of powdered sanderswood, and 1 part each of nitre, oil of sandalwood, cinnamon, and cloves. Make into a paste with a solution of gum tragacanth (made by pouring 6 parts of warm water over 1 part of gum tragacanth, letting it stand a few days and then straining), and form into cones.

To make Aromatic Pastils. Another Recipe.—Mix together 125 parts of charcoal, 25 parts each of cascarilla bark and gum benzoin, 12 parts of nitre, 10 parts of myrrh, and 5 parts each of oil of cloves and oil of nutmeg. Make into a paste with a solution of gum tragacanth.

FURNITURE Polish.—Mix together one pint of linseed oil, half a pint of vinegar, and two table-spoonfuls of turpentine. Rub it well in with a flannel, and then thoroughly polish with a duster. Never leave the furniture sticky, but rub it till it is quite bright and clean.

The best polish for oak is made by melting a pound of beeswax in a pint of turpentine. It must be used when it is of the consistency of dripping.

If a polished table or tray has been marked by a hot dish, cover the place with beeswax and turpentine mixed together, and leave it for one hour. Then rub off the beeswax with a leather. Should the hot dish have scorched the wood, darken the place with a little linseed oil, and then polish it.

For brass, use Putz' German Pomade. Rub it well on, and then polish the brass thoroughly with a leather.—*J. R.*

To destroy the Smell of Paint in Rooms.—Place in each room a pail of water in which two or three handfuls of hay are immersed. At the end of six hours the hay will have absorbed much of the smell of the paint. Burn the hay, throw away the water, and repeat the process as often as required.—*J. R.*

To destroy Flies.—Take half a tea-spoonful of freshly ground black pepper, a tea-spoonful of brown sugar, and a tea-spoonful of cream. Mix all well together, and put it on a plate. The flies in the room will soon disappear.—*J. R.*

To destroy Black Beetles.—The Union Cockroach Paste, invented by Mr. Howarth, F.Z.S., for use in the workhouse at Sheffield when it was infested with black beetles, never fails in its effect. It is sold in tins by Mr. Hewitt, Chemist, 66, Division Street, Sheffield.—*J. R.*

To make a Cement for China or Glass.—Mix thoroughly two and a half ounces of white of egg with one ounce of finely powdered quicklime, carefully adding an ounce of water and five and a half ounces of plaster of Paris. This cement should be used as soon as made.

To make Stick½fast Paste.—Dissolve a quarter of a pound of gum arabic in half a pint of water, and carefully mix therewith an ounce of sugar and three ounces of starch. Heat in a water-bath till it becomes clear. Add half a dram of oil of cloves and allow to cool.

To make Baking-powder. — Mix together ten ounces of bicarbonate of soda, eight ounces of tartaric acid, and a pound of corn-flour, ground-rice, or wheat-flour. Thoroughly mix the powders, pass through a sieve, and store.

It is essential that the several materials used in the preparation of baking-powder shall be separately fire-dried with thoroughness previously to being mixed. The presence of the smallest quantity of dampness renders the mixture quite inoperative. Baking-powder should therefore be carefully stored in air-tight boxes or bins.

To keep Cut Flowers fresh, they should be supplied with fresh water every morning, when also a tiny bit of the end of the stem should be cut off and the whole stem gently wiped with a cloth. No leaves should be left on that part of the stem which is under water.

ABSINTHE, 104
Ale, 71–76
  ,,   cup, 117
  ,,   mulled, 122
Anchovy sauce, 47
Angostura bitters, 112
Aniseed cordial, 105

BACON, PICKLE FOR, 28
Badminton, 117
Balm of Molucca, 112
Baking-powder, 150
Beauty water, 96
Beef, spiced, 24
  ,,   tea, 139
  ,,   Welsh, 25
Beer, home-brewed, 71–76
Beetles, to destroy, 153
Benedictine, 115
Biscuits, water, 136
Bishop, 117
Bitters, angostura, 112
  ,,   Hamburgh, 106
  ,,   orange, 115
Boston cooler, 118
Bottling of fruit and vegetables, 63–66
Brandy, cherry, 113
  ,,   cherries, 55
  ,,   cocktail, 118
  ,,   ginger, 114
  ,,   lemon, 114
  ,,   peaches, 56
Brewing, 71–76
Broth, 139, 140

Browning, gush about, 2
Butter, 9–15
  ,,   to pot, 14

CALVES'-FOOT JELLY, 142
Cassis, 113
Catsup, mushroom, 45
  ,,   tomato, 46
  ,,   walnut, 46
Champagne cobbler, 113
  ,,   cup, 118
Chartreuse, 106
Cheese, 16–22
  ,,   Camembert, 21
  ,,   Cheddar, 18
  ,,   cream, 19
  ,,   Gervais, 21
  ,,   Grewelthorp, 20
  ,,   Stilton, 16
  ,,   to pot, 22
Cherries, brandy, 55
Cherry brandy, 113
Churning, 12
Cider, 77–79
  ,,   cup, 118
Cinnamon cordial, 106
Claret cup, 118
  ,,   mulled, 123
Clove cordial, 106
Cobbett, William, on pietistic and other cant, 71–73
Cobbler, champagne, 118
  ,,   Saratoga, 125
  ,,   sherry, 126
Cocktail, brandy, 118

Coffee, 119, 136
Cordials, 102–116
Crambambuli, 120
Cream, 9–15
   ,,   clotted, 11
   ,,   curds, 15
Crême de cacao, 113
   ,,   ,, café, 113
   ,,   ,, menthe, 114
Crust coffee, 143
Curaçoa, 114
Curry powder, 45
Custard, savoury, 141
Cutlet, mutton, 140

DAMSON CHEESE, 55
Distilling, 92–111
Drying of fruit and vegetables, 67–70

EAU-DE-COLOGNE, 145
Egg-and-brandy mixture, 120
Egg flip, 120
   ,, nog,'120
Eggs, to preserve, 32
Essences, 96–102
Evaporating of fruit and vegetables, 67–70

FILBERTS, STORING OF, 62
Fish, to pickle, 31
   ,, to pot, 30
   ,, to salt, 31
   ,, to smoke, 31
Flies, to destroy, 149
Flowers, cut, to keep fresh, 151
Fruit, bottling of, 63–66
   ,, drink, 121
   ,, drying of, 67–70
   ,, Macédoine, 130
   ,, storing, 57–62
   ,, syrups, 65
Furniture polish, 149

GARDEN PARTY, REFRESHMENTS AT, 128–136

Gin fizz, 121
   ,, punch, 124
   ,, sling, 121
Ginger beer, 89
   ,, brandy, 114
Gingerbread loaf, 135

HAM, 26
   ,, to boil, 28
   ,, to cure, 27
   ,, to steam, 29
Hamburgh bitters, 108
Henry VIII., appreciator of pudding, 2
Herbs, gathering and drying, 62
Housewifery, a plea for, 1–8
Hughes, Tom, on life, beer and skittles, 117
Hydromel, 89

ICE CREAMS, 137, 138
Incense, 147
Invalids, food for, 139–144

JAMS, 48–56
Jellies, fruit, 52
Jelly, apple, 52
   ,, blackberry, 54
   ,, cranberry, 53
   ,, currant, 53, 54
   ,, Scotch, 54
   ,, calves'-foot, 142
   ,, restorative, 141
   ,, rice, 142
Julep, 122

KING, DR., HIS APPEAL TO THE ALE-WIFE, 76
Kirschenwasser, 108
Kummel, 108

LA MASUBAL, 121
Lavender, gathering and drying, 62
   ,, water, 96, 146
Lemon brandy, 114

Lemon cordial, 111, 114
Lemonade, 121
Long drink, 121

MACÉDOINE OF FRUIT, 130
Markham, Gervase, on the vertues
    of a complete woman, 6
Marmalade, crab-apple, 52
    ,,   orange, 50, 51
    ,,   quince, 51
Mead, 87–89
Meat, pickling, 23–30
  ,,   to pot, 30
Medlars, storing of, 61
Merissah, 87
Metheglin, 87–89
Milk, 9–15
  ,,   punch, 123
Mint julep, 122
Mulled ale, 122
    ,,   claret, 123
Mushroom catsup, 45
Mustard, 40
    ,,   aromatic, 42
    ,,   Düsseldorf, 42
    ,,   Frankfort, 42
    ,,   French, 41
    ,,   Jesuits', 42
    ,,   spiced, 41
    ,,   with horseradish, 40

NOYAU, 111

ORANGE BITTERS, 115
    ,,   cordial, 111

PAINT, TO REMOVE THE SMELL OF,
    149
Pastils, aromatic, 148
Paste, stick-fast, 150
Peaches, brandy, 56
Perfumes, 145–148
Pickle for bacon, 28
Pickling apples, 38
    ,,   apricots, 38
    ,,   barberries, 38

Pickling bean pods, 38
    ,,   beetroot, 38
    ,,   cabbage, 34
    ,,   cauliflower, 38
    ,,   damsons, 38
    ,,   fish, 31
    ,,   gherkins, 36
    ,,   meat, 23–30
    ,,   mushrooms, 38
    ,,   nasturtium seeds, 37
    ,,   onions, 38
    ,,   peaches, 38
    ,,   pears, 38
    ,,   plums, 37
    ,,   samphire, 37
    ,,   shallots, 34
    ,,   tomatoes, 36, 37
    ,,   vegetables, 33–39
    ,,   walnuts, 36
Picnic, refreshments at, 128–136
Pigs' cheeks, to cure, 28
Polish, for furniture, etc., 149
Potting fish, 30
    ,,   meat, 30
    ,,   shrimps, 31
Pot-pourri, 145
Preserves, 48–56
Punch, 123, 124
Purl, 124

RASPBERRY VINEGAR, 125
Rice jelly, 142
Rosemary water, 96
Rum shrub, 115

SANDWICHES, 128–132
Sauce, anchovy, 47
    ,,   piquant, 46, 47
Sauerkraut, 38
Salad dressing, 47
Saratoga cobbler, 125
Sausages, to cook, 26
    ,,   to make, 25
Scent-bags, 146
Shandy-gaff, 125
Sherbet, 125

Index

Sherry cobbler, 126
Shrimps, to pot, 31
Shrub brandy, 112
  „ rum, 115
Sighs of love, 115
Sloe gin, 116
Spiced beef, 24
Spruce, beer, 90
Storing of fruit and herbs, 57–62
Sweet-jar, 145
Swift, on the necessity of cordials, 112
Syllabub, 126

TEA, COLD, 133–135
Tent, 116
Tewahdiddle, 126
Toast and water, 143
Tomato catsup, 46

USQUEBAUGH, 116

VEGETABLES, BOTTLING OF, 63–66
  „   drying of, 67–70

Vermouth, 116
Vinegar, toilet, 146
  „   aromatic, for smelling bottles, 142
  „   aromatic table, 44, 45
  „   spiced table, 44

WALNUTS, STORING OF, 62
Walnut catsup, 46
Wassail, 126
Water biscuits, 136
Waters, aromatic, 96
Welsh beef, 25
Wine, cowslip, 86
  „   damson, 87
  „   date, 87
  „   elderberry, 90
  „   gooseberry, 85
  „   lemon, 86
  „   making, 80–91
  „   rhubarb, 87
Wines, aromatic, 45

YORKSHIRE PUDDING, 141

HANDBOOKS
of Practical Gardening
Under the General Editorship of
HARRY ROBERTS

Price 2s. 6d. *net. Crown 8vo. Cloth. Illustrated. Price* $1.00 *net.*

VOL.
I. THE BOOK OF ASPARAGUS. By C. Ilott, F.R.H.S.

II. THE BOOK OF THE GREENHOUSE. By J. C. Tallack, F.R.H.S.

III. THE BOOK OF THE GRAPE. By H. W. Ward, F.R.H.S.

IV. THE BOOK OF OLD-FASHIONED FLOWERS. By Harry Roberts.

V. THE BOOK OF BULBS. By S. Arnott, F.R.H.S.

VI. THE BOOK OF THE APPLE. By H. H. Thomas.

VII. THE BOOK OF VEGETABLES. By G. Wythes, V.M.N.

VIII. THE BOOK OF ORCHIDS. By W. H. White, F.R.H.S.

IX. THE BOOK OF THE STRAWBERRY. By E. Beckett, F.R.H.S.

X. THE BOOK OF CLIMBING PLANTS. By S. Arnott, F.R.H.S.

XI. THE BOOK OF PEARS AND PLUMS. By the Rev. E. Bartrum, D.D.

XII. THE BOOK OF HERBS. By Lady Rosalind Northcote.

XIII. THE BOOK OF THE WILD GARDEN. By S. W. Fitzherbert.

XIV. THE BOOK OF THE HONEY BEE. By C. Harrison.

XV. THE BOOK OF SHRUBS. By G. Gordon, V.M.H.

XVI. THE BOOK OF THE DAFFODIL. By the Rev. S. E. Bourne.

XVII. THE BOOK OF THE LILY. By W. Goldring.

XVIII. THE BOOK OF TOPIARY. By W. Gibson and Charles H. Curtis.

XIX. THE BOOK OF TOWN AND WINDOW GARDENING. By Mrs F. A. Bardswell.

XX. THE BOOK OF RARER VEGETABLES. By George Wythes.

XXI. THE BOOK OF THE IRIS.

XXII. THE BOOK OF GARDEN FURNITURE.

*** *Any of the above volumes will be sent post free by a bookseller on receipt of a postal order for two shillings and ninepence.*

The Country Handbooks

A Series of Illustrated Practical Handbooks dealing with Country Life, suitable for the Pocket or Knapsack

Under the General Editorship of
HARRY ROBERTS

Price 3s. net, bound in Limp Cloth.   Price $1.00 net.
Price 4s. net. bound in Limp Leather.   Price $1.20 net.

Vol. I.—THE TRAMP'S HANDBOOK. *For the use of Travellers, Soldiers, Cyclists, and lovers of the Country. By Harry Roberts.*

A volume written in defence of vagabondage, containing much valuable advice to the amateur gypsy, traveller, or cyclist, as to camping-out, cooking, &c.

Vol. II.—THE MOTOR BOOK. *By R. J. Mecredy.*

An invaluable handbook that should find a place in the library of every motorist, or even in the car itself.

Vol. III.—THE BIRD BOOK. *By A. J. R. Roberts.*

A guide to the study of bird life, with hints as to recognising various species by their flight or their note.

Vol. IV.—THE STILL ROOM. *By Mrs Charles Roundell.*

A book full of information upon all subjects pertaining to preserving, pickling, bottling, distilling, &c.; with many useful hints upon the dairy.

Vol. V.—THE TREE BOOK. *By Mary Rowles Jarvis.*

Containing varied and useful information relating to forests, together with a special chapter on Practical Forestry.

Vol. VI.—THE WOMAN OUT OF DOORS. *By Ménie Muriel Dowie.*

Vol. VII.—THE HORSEMAN'S HANDBOOK. *By William Foster.*

Vol. VIII.—THE FISHERMAN'S HANDBOOK. *By Edgar S. Shrubsole.*

An Eight-page Prospectus Post Free on Application.

COUNCIL

Hon. H. A. STANHOPE, *President.*

Captain J. N. PRESTON, *Vice Pres.* | STANES CHAMBERLAYNE, Esq.
W. H. WHITAKER, Esq. | EGBERT DE HAMEL, Esq.
EDWARD OWEN GREENING, Esq., *Managing Director.*
EDWARD W. GREENING, Esq , *Secretary.*

RELIABLE PRODUCTIONS OF THE ASSOCIATION

"ONE & ALL" SPECIAL OILCAKES FOR CATTLE:—No. 1, Dairy Cake for Milk Production ; No. 2, Feeding Cake for Young Stock ; No. 3, Fatting Cake for Rapid Fattening ; No. 4, Store Cake for Summer Feed. "One & All" Linseed and Decorticated Cotton Cakes. "One & All" Milk Meal for Calves. "One & All" Condiment, a pure spice for cattle, horses, etc.

"ONE & ALL" COMPLETE FERTILISERS FOR FARM AND GARDEN, properly proportioned for different crops and varying soils.

"ONE & ALL" SEEDS FOR FARM AND GARDEN of the highest excellence and purity.

Catalogues Post Free on Application.

PUBLICATIONS OF THE AGRICULTURAL AND HORTICULTURAL ASSOCIATION, LTD.

THE "AGRICULTURAL ECONOMIST."—An Illustrated Art Magazine of Agriculture, Horticulture, and Co-operation. Published monthly. Price 6d., or 5s. per annum, post free. Specimen Copy free on application.

"'ONE & ALL' GARDENING."—A popular Annual for Amateurs, Allotment Holders, and Working Gardeners. About 200 pages, profusely illustrated. Price 2d , all booksellers.

"VEGETABLE AND FLOWER SEEDS."—Free by post on application.
"FARM SEEDS."—Free by post on application.
"ARTIFICIAL FERTILISERS."—Free by post on application.
"FEEDING STUFFS."—Free by post on application.

The Book Department of the Association supplies all Works on Farming and Gardening.
All details respecting the Association and its operations sent post free on application to

Edwd Owen Greening

Managing Director.

CENTRAL OFFICES & WHOLESALE SEED WAREHOUSES:
92 LONG ACRE, LONDON, W.C.

OILCAKE MILL & MANURE WORKS:
"ONE & ALL" WHARF, GREEK ROAD, DEPTFORD, LONDON, S.E.

By CHARLES HENRY LANE

ALL ABOUT DOGS. A Book for Doggy People. With 85 full-page Illustrations (including nearly 70 champions) by R. H. Moore.

Price 7s. 6d. net. Demy 8vo. Price $2.50 net.

"One of the most interesting contributions to the literature of the day."—*Daily Chronicle.*

"Mr Lane's book is worthy of a place on the shelves of any sporting library."—*Outlook.*

"A most interesting, indeed, an entirely fascinating book."—*St James's Gazette.*

"A mine of information."—*Fur and Feather.*

"To be read from cover to cover."—*Country Gentleman.*

"The 'points,' in competitions, are set forth as becomes a practised judge; the remarks on treatment and disease are practical and brief; the illustrations are good and spirited."—*Athenæum.*

"Every breed is taken and described on a plan that is full and satisfactory, while the Doggy Stories will tickle everybody's palate!"—*Sportsman.*

"The advice he gives to exhibitors is invaluable, coming from one *who has almost an unrivalled record as a judge.* Dog lovers of every degree should hasten to possess themselves of this excellent handbook."—*Pall Mall Gazette.*

"C. H. Lane, whose knowledge of dogs is extensive and peculiar, has written a book about dogs which is *absolutely the most fascinating we have ever read.* Everyone who loves dogs should treat himself, or herself, to a copy of this excellent volume!"—*Star.*

"With this book as a guide the uninitiated cannot go far wrong and even the specialist may learn."—*Echo.*

JOHN LANE, PUBLISHER, LONDON & NEW YORK

Boston Public Library
Central Library, Copley Square

Division of
Reference and Research Services